Beneath a Magic Sky

by

Douglas A. Cox

Beneath a Magic Sky
Douglas A. Cox
1000 N. Green Valley Parkway
Suite 440-392
Henderson, NV 89074
United States of America
www.DougCoxOnline.com
Email: DougCox22@cox.net

Cover Photo by Keith Kirk
Editing by Sharon Norman
Layout & Design by Linda A. Bell

BIOGRAPHY & AUTOBIOGRAPHY/personal memoirs/sunlight and shadows/Douglas A. Cox -1st. ed.

ISBN: 9798317239190

Printed in the United States of America

Disclaimer
The purpose of this book is to educate, motivate, and inspire. The author shall have neither liability nor responsibility to any person or entity with respect to any loss or damage caused or alleged to be caused directly or indirectly by the information contained in this book.

CONTENTS

Beneath 6

Absent 8

Drums 10

Lightfall 12

First Down 14

Harbinger 16

Windy 18

Wormhole (Colorado) 20

When Down is Up 22

The Blambet 24

Midnight Train 26

Regrets 28

Armor 30

Bubbles 32

Mom 34

Brilliant! 36

Asclepius 38

Click 40

Evening Primrose 42

Honeysuckle 44

Brothers! 46

Key Largo 48

Marv (Part One) 50

Marv (Part Two) 52

The Porch 54

Fire 56

Gear 58

Is That Your Kite? 60

On the Nose 62

Sing 64

Tables 66

Moments 68

The Club 70
The Tree 72
Sleeping Out 74
Turquoise 76
Jazz 78
Tolstoy 80
Wilson 82
Ice Cream 84
One Special Evening 86
The Trestle (Part One) 88
The Trestle (Part Two) 90
The Trestle (Part Three) 92
The Trestle (Part Four) 94
Spellbound 96
Bill 98
The Call of Autumn 100
Without a Song! 102
Word Painter 104
The Battle at Glenwood 106
Friends 108
Grateful 110
Accents 112
Contact 114
Lost 116
Magic 118
Bemelmans Bar 120
Eagles (Part One) 122
Eagles (Part Two) 124
Bats 126
Football 128
The Trickster 130
Discoveries 132
El Pipo 134
Compose 136
Gone Away 138
High Rise 140

The Blue Bar 142
The Sycamores 144
Wright-Rite-Right 146
Smile 148
The Chase 150
The Havest 152
Metamorphosis 154
Bob 156
Neighbors and the Universe 158
Toast 160
Tandem 162
A Face in the Crowd 164
One Day 166
Magic Carpet (Part One) 168
Magic Carpet (Part Two) 170
Magic Carpet (Part Three) 172
Magic Carpet (Part Four) 174
Magic Carpet (Part Five) 176
Peace 178

Beneath

Hello and welcome to the campfire. We live our lives here on earth, laughing, crying, living, and dying beneath this wonderful magic sky. Blazing sun or winter night, I love the experience of being outdoors and simply looking up to see what the great spirit has prepared for me. At our home, on Coyote Road, in Montecito, California, we had a special place up the hill we called the Christopher Robin Meadow. It was a reserved spot for fairy tales, storytelling, sharing adventures, and sky gazing.

This wonderful meadow was our place for the discussion of spiritual things. Any questions or thoughts that our offspring had, regarding God, religion, or faith, were shared here. No question was off limits, no subject was out of bounds and my kids, being extremely bright, often had me heading back down the hill to do my homework, in preparation for our next council. I would simply wait for our brood to fall asleep and then step out on the front porch to sit in silence, look up through the giant old oak at the Sacred Sky and ask for guidance as it related to the deeper questions of life and divinity.

I sure do love the way that you worship, and I would fight to the death to protect your right to do so. As a cowboy, I have found that the great outdoors has always been my cathedral. Having lived so many years, I have come to know the Chairman of the

Board well and this is the best place to go to chat with him. I so do love and admire my children for their independence and faith. Each is so different. Each so true and focused. We have spent so many family days and nights beneath this sacred sky. Sometimes chatting, often just resting in silence, each in our own world of thought.

Whatever these wonderful people have chosen for their life's path, they have grown to be honest and loving. They are excellent wives, husbands, sons, and daughters. They are or will become excellent grandparents. They are true to their beliefs and marvelous representatives of the Desert Wind. Now, it is time to share some stories, Beneath a Magic Sky.

Blest, Tigger

Absent

Can it be that we humans are connected in a very deep and spiritual way? The voice in my soul spoke softly, "Contact Nanook... Now!" So, I did. From his hospital bed he asked, "did you know that I was in here?" My answer was, "no, just felt you calling."

"Have you been half asleep and have you heard voices?" Those wonderful words are from the Academy Award winning song composed by Kenneth Ascher and Paul Williams. The song was performed in the Muppet Movie by Kermit the Frog.

(Movie Scene...) The bus is broken down in the California desert. Beneath a clear starry southwestern sky, Kermit and his friends are sharing a campfire. What a joy to be stuck with dear friends. "There's not a word yet for old friends who've just met." A harmonica, guitar and Gonzo to remind us: "You can just visit but I plan to stay... I'm going to go back there someday."

Paul Williams is a great songwriter. He is also a great guy. When asked about his inspiration for the Academy Award Winning composition "Rainbow Connection," he invoked the names of Fred and Ms. Rogers and then exclaimed, "The Elements of Kindness!" You don't have to look far if you know Fred Rogers and Jim Henson, to find kindness in both word and deed.

How can it be, with all of the prayers and proclamations, that we can find our way to being so mean spirited? "I want this, so I will do anything to get it." Run over anyone, step on anyone, harm anyone and fly in the face of the tenets of our self- proclaimed faith, to get our way. I have known Nanook, "Rick" Thornton for more than fifty years. I am sure that it is our mutual respect and common kindness that connects us so surely.

Many of us must have been absent the day they were presenting the class on kindness. May we all reawaken the power of kindness with which we were bestowed at birth. At last, we would all make the Rainbow Connection...

Tigger

Drums

I remember… It was my eighteenth birthday and my mom had something special planned. The big reveal came when I walked home from my high school and swung open the front door. There before me was a brand new, beautiful, "green sparkle" set of Slingerland drums. It was a Gene Krupa deluxe set, with bright shiny Zildjian Symbols and sticks, at the ready. When my mom did it, she did it right. She even included a cat! At least there was a cat sitting on my drummer's stool… It was our wonderful family cat "Wooley."

The drum set came with a few stipulations. One: I was to take care of it like I loved it. Two: I was to take lessons and learn to play properly if not professionally. And three: I was to pass on what I learned to others interested in the art of drumming. I have kept my word. My teacher, in Pasadena, California, so I am told, was the best in the business. He gave very careful, inspired instruction and expected practice and crisp demonstration on the following weeks' lesson. I truly did my best.

There are rewards for discipline. Over these many years, I have not only remembered some of the rudiments but continue to practice them in an unusual way. I drum with my hands on anything I can find, my legs, tables, and my practice pad. You can play too: A triplet goes Right-Left-Right and then reverses to Left-Right-

Left. I still lay it down the way I was taught, increasing the speed until I slip up and then start over. I remember a paradiddle... Sounds like two-diddles but it plays out R-L-R-R and reverses to L-R-L-L. Single stroke rolls are also a great practice. (R-L-R-L-R-L-R-L.) As the days and years pass by and things seem to slow down a bit, I have found this practice puts my mind and body in a rhythm that thinks, plays, and remembers, like an eighteen-year-old. Won't *you* give it a try?

It was on stage at my high school, in Altadena California, that I had the gift of fulfilling my promise. With Joanne Grogan on piano, Pete Applan on sax, Herbie Lewis on bass, and yours truly on drums... We won the John Muir talent contest and went on to take top honors in the Pasadena City talent revue.

Thanks mom,
Tigger

Lightfall

Southern California afternoons are often glorious and this one did not disappoint. It was a beautiful wedding at the old mission, in San Gabriel. The bride's hair was regal and shiny black, as it moved ever so graciously in the breeze. The groom's dark hair was a fine contrast to his white dinner jacket, and he appeared chiseled and handsome in front of the gathered guests. It was a special day and a dream for a photographer.

As you may know, I walk every day. Sometimes up the mountain, often up two mountains and then again, I walk our neighborhood in search of treasure. Trusty camera slung over my shoulder, I am a prospector looking for wonders, both great and small. Butterflies, bugs, birds, lizards, flowers, and anything that creeps, crawls, flies, or grows in our mysterious desert, is on my photo menu.

This week, on just such a sojourn, I spotted a rose bush truly covered with colorful blossoms. As I approached this radiant beauty, I began snapping away. First the large picture of the whole artwork and then ever closer I began to try and determine which blossoms would be my solo targets.

After all of the one-hundred-thousand-plus images I have captured, I realized that it was second nature to me, to choose the part of the object upon which I should focus. So, it was during this thinking game I play with myself, that it came to me. It was the *"lightfall"* on the object that drew me in and begged me to click the shutter and so capture one blossom in a million.

I love discoveries, particularly about myself and my living. I have a terrific friend, in Florida, who is a great and accomplished photographer. Denis' work with world champion teams and athletes is renowned. So, when he takes a moment to Facebook me, to share that one of my captures found his favor, I am honored and appreciative. I now know the answer...It's the lightfall!

Tigger

First Down

This pandemic has sure enough changed our world. I enjoy asking family, friends, and clients, how it has affected their lives and the answers are interesting. First of all, old Tigger is such a positive cat, that I would never ask for the negative version of their answers but that is what I get. I hate the doctors, I hate the school board, I hate the politicians, and I hate my neighbors. I hate the masked and the unmasked, I hate the vaxed and the unvaxed. My goodness... I just love everybody and try to respect their views and mind my own beeswax!

Here's the good news, I love football. One Covid catch for me is, I don't like watching the games alone. I have the best friends who are living out the pandemic, right and proper, sticking to their beliefs and protecting their neighbors and I admire them for that. Now Frank and John and I hop on that iPhone the moment we see, or the announcer mentions a *"scamper..."* That is a good long run from either team, which leads to a first down or a touchdown.

My wife loves to watch! Not football but department store shelves while I am watching football, alone. So last Christmas she brought home a sweet little gift box and presented it to me at one of my lonely half-times. Once opened, the tissue paper revealed the cutest little stuffed puppy dog or puffed stuppy dog if you've been drinking. He was a little black and white rascal and I grabbed him up and gave him a great big hug. That was when I realized how much I missed those. Hugs that is.

Of course, as we do with everything from cars to pets, we had to find him a name. We wanted something that would include him in our celebrations. I chose *"First Down..."* It just seemed right at the time. It gave us a chance to celebrate our new little friend, whenever our team made a first down! Then we could cheer for our team and hate our opponents. Or whatever.

Go Pooh Team...
Tigger

Harbinger

I remember a chilly morning in Carmel, California. The fog had crawled in from the mighty pacific and rolled up the streets, filling the doorways with thick, moist cotton candy. It was an Eastwood kind of day. Clint had picked up his newspaper at the Carmel Drug Store and as his pickup truck pulled away, we waved good morning and I turned to walk across the street... Important business!

It could be London or Liverpool, but this was wondrous Carmel-by-the-Sea. I was heading to the Harbinger restaurant in the Carmel Plaza to meet my friend Mike. This restaurant on the courtyard was our dreaming, thinking, planning place.

The young server nodded, smiled, and placed our fine California Chardonnay on the table. She had seen us coming. She knew us both, as Mike was a farmer from the valley and my home was in Carmel Highlands just down the road. Turn south on 101 and head on to Mal Paso and then right onto Yankee Point Drive. In two shakes of a lamb's tail, a fragrant hot plate of steamed rice with freshly harvested veggies was before us. Of course, we could sit inside on such a day, but this was our table, and this was our time.

Websters Dictionary tells us that a "Harbinger" is a person or thing that announces the approach of another. To me it has always represented a beautiful bird, who arrives to share with us the good news yet to come. If I listen very carefully, through the morning fog, I can hear the message: "This virus will be defeated, and we will hug our family and loved ones once again." The economy of our wonderful nation will, slowly but surely return and we will be invited to contribute to its wealth through our labors. Our children, both grand and great grand, will return to school and to the relationships that build them into the wonders they will become.

I believe in the possibilities, and I believe in us!

Tigger

Windy

The wind that blows across the vast southwestern part of the United States can bring with it, the most dramatic mysteries that hold observers spell bound. From still and tender as a newborns' breath, to as loud and violent as a screaming banshee, the desert wind is an opera all of its own.

This season, it has played its part in creating weather wonders as dynamic as any I have ever experienced in the Las Vegas Valley. Morning is often the quiet time, with air so still, that one can capture the fragrance of each of the various individual shrubs along the pathway. Evening can bring straight-line winds of fifty to sixty miles an hour, which can carry the smell of Sierra pine and now and then, the distant but mighty Pacific Ocean. We are used to three to four such days a season but 2021 has proven to be a record breaker, with day after day of window rattling wind.

Depending on which direction the pressure gradient system driven winds, enter and cross our valley, the dust comes along with them and makes for some interesting views. We often share an evening cocktail on our patio, enjoying the twinkling city lights below. Imagine our surprise when we walked out, beverage in hand, only to find that the City of Las Vegas had completely disappeared! We certainly enjoy some of the greatest magic in the world, but this dust storm topped them all.

The thing that impresses me most about this windy season, is what this gusty business brings out in our neighbors. On trash day afternoon, preparing to head out on the street to pick up windblown trash and trash cans, I saw that my across the street neighbor had beaten me to the punch. He was out there lifting the cans and moving them up the driveways and against the garages.

I believe in folks, and they often validate my belief!

Tigger

Wormhole (Colorado)

On the patio of Chris and Janie's home in Denver Colorado, beneath a crystal clear and starry sky, we stepped into a time warp. With a handful of friends, a fine cocktail and a down jacket, we cashed in our "E" tickets to a portal, opening up both head and heart. We were carried aloft by the many gifts of artists and composers whose ability to transport, is legendary. Past, present, and future, one-by-one, we each chose a recording to share and together we committed ourselves to opening our hearts, revisiting the reveries and journeys of the others. What a trip!

Where was it? When was it, and what were the words that swept you away and held you spellbound? I wrote just recently, that a song is the greatest time machine. Anywhere, any-when and any-how, we can be transported!

The incomparable Trisha Yearwood, "The Song Remembers When," might well have been our theme song. The composer, Hugh Prestwood, starts us off in a store where, *"I heard that old familiar music start..."* From there to the Rocky Mountains, high above the clouds and on to the heart awakening chorus, *"And even though the whole world has forgotten, the Song Remembers When."*

Antonio Carlos Jobim, next, flew us to the beach, in Brazil: *"I who was lost and lonely, believing life was only a bitter tragic joke, have found with you, the meaning of existence, Oh my love."*

Fred Neil was our next navigator. I picture him sitting on a tall barstool in a Florida beach-front pub, foot tapping rhythm and his mysterious baritone voice, surrounded by his rich twelve strung guitar, just putting it out there: *"I only know that peace will come when all hate is gone, and I been searchin' for the dolphins livin' in the sea..."* And then he adds: *"Sometimes I wonder if you ever think of me."* Where do you go when you head into the wormhole?

Tigger

When Down is Up

Carried by the warm summer wind, their down drifts easily beneath an azure sky. Above our desert, they float on their way to becoming a landing strip and diner for an endangered butterfly. Celebrating a flash of youth and vigor, I run to catch the magic fluff that carries with it, the seed that is the milkweed. Therein rides the sustenance for the next generation of beautiful bright orange and black butterflies.

Milkweed is the host plant for the monarch. Without milkweed the larva would not be able develop into a butterfly. The nectar in all milkweed flowers provides valuable food for butterflies, bees, and other pollinators. Butterflies not only need nectar, but they also need food at the caterpillar stage. The leaves of the milkweed plant are the only food that monarch butterflies can eat and with their unique chemistry, the toxicity gives them a very unpleasant taste to predators. Their lovely colors send an extremely specific message. "Don't eat me, I taste terrible!"

"The Butterfly Trees," is a documentary feature film, that traces the transcontinental journey of the eastern monarchs on their epic migration, from the forested shores of southern Canada, to the rare and ancient oyamel fir trees of central Mexico.

My trees are the Butterfly Sanctuary of Pacific Grove, California.

Meet me there at Thanksgiving and we will share the blessing.

The birthplace of the monarch is a striking caterpillar, yellow, black, and white; whose chrysalis produces a joyful surprise. As Lao Tzu spoke: "What the caterpillar calls the end, the rest of the world calls a butterfly!"

"And away they all flew, like the down of a thistle..."

Tigger

The Blambet

The fireplace is crackling, the music is soft and low, and hot chocolate with marshmallows, tastes delicious. The woodsmoke smells like heaven and the blambet is pulled up snug around our chin.

What? You have never heard of a blambet? Can it be, that you have come this far without crossing paths with this magic device? Our dear friends shared with us, their family pronunciation, "Blambet" for the word blanket. Winter, as we all know, can bring a huge range of reports. In Fort Lauderdale, a morning dip along the shore, may mean fifty-two degrees in the air, with a balmy seventy-four-degree water temp. Please hold my towel ready.

For our treasured friend Nanook, in Alaska, it means a twelve degree wake up and a twenty-degree hustle across the parking lot, for lunch at La Mex.

In our southwestern desert, cold probably means a twenty-nine-degree morning with a fifty-degree afternoon up on Doug's Mountain.

When British weaver Thomas Kay arrived in Oregon, in 1863, he laid the foundation of the Pendleton Woolen Mills that we know today. When Kay's three grandsons, the Bishop Brothers, joined him in the early 1900's, they brought their native American inspired designs into the Pendleton Trade blanket. The color and designs of the blankets and robes were very popular with the local Nez Perce, and soon the Navajo, Hopi, and Zuni nations, found favor in the beautiful woven fabrics of Pendleton. The blankets soon became a standard of value, for trading and credit among Native Americans.

On a warm summer evening we drove out to the Taos pueblo, in New Mexico. We were visiting with an old family friend, Augustine Mirabal, who was part of the Leadership Team for the Tribe. In our arms, we brought a gift of gratitude to share with Augustine and his wife, a beautiful, warm "Chief's Robe" Pendleton Blambet. They loved it and we were honored.

Tigger

Midnight Train

I loved my time in radio and records. It was a blessing to share and a window into a thousand people, songs, stories, and magic. I have found that following the trail of a hit song, might well lead to a marvelous adventure.

"He started playing his guitar, and I started humming and it was magic..." If I told you who "he" was, there is a very good chance that you would have no idea who I'm writing about. He was a football player for the University of Mississippi where, with him as quarterback, the team went undefeated in 1962 and won both the SEC and National championships. But his life took a different turn after college, leading him to become a part of our lives.

Moving to Los Angeles he took up flag football and ended up playing ball with TV actor Lee Majors of the "Million Dollar Man." One day he phoned Lee at home and reached Lee's girlfriend. They chatted for a moment, and she mentioned that she was about to take the midnight plane to Houston. A bell went off in the songwriter side of his mind. The voice on the phone was of course the actress who ended up being a Charlie's Angel. That's right, a casual comment by Farrah Fawcett-Majors ended up being the inspiration for a Hall of Fame song, "Midnight Train to Georgia." One of Rolling Stone's 500 greatest songs of all time.

Originally penned as a country song, the Grammy winning "Midnight Train," turned out to be just one of a number of hits written by Jim Weatherly, who along with Gladys Knight recorded "Neither One of Us Wants to be the First to Say Goodbye," and "The Best Thing That Ever Happened to Me."

Music is a wonderful time machine! Check out "The Need to Be," by Jim.

Thank you, Gladys, the Pips, and rest in Peace J.W.

Tigger

Regrets

I had gone to visit a longtime friend who was recovering from some health challenges. When she saw the red and raw condition of my face, she gasped and asked if that was the result of skin cancer? My answer: "kind of…" My hesitation was not trying to avoid the truth. It was my wanting to share the whole story.

After living most of my life out of doors and in the sunlight, I have had way more than my share of solar exposure. The resulting radiation and damage, has left me with a rather serious case of skin cancer. My various diagnoses have included three common types of carcinoma: actinic keratosis, basal cell, and squamous cell. It has been my good fortune and blessing not to be visited by melanoma, the bad boy of skin cancers.

My Mohs Surgeons have estimated that I have had about a thousand sutures or stitches in my body. In the beginning, almost every exam and the resulting diagnosis, required surgery to remove the lesions that appeared on a regular basis. So where is the good news? With care, use of sunscreen and, proper dress for my current constant outdoor activities, I and my dermatology team have helped me avoid surgery for the last three years. By exposing my face to a specific type of radiation, called blue light, I am able to reduce the frequency and seriousness of my eruptions. I do look like a roast turkey for a couple of weeks, but the absence of surgery is a blessed gift.

Observing my recently treated face, as I dropped my Covid mask, my friend asked, "Don't you regret spending all that time in the sun?" My answer came out instantly. "I wouldn't trade one glorious ride on my White Owl surfboard or one beautiful afternoon on the southern California sand. If I could change anything, it would be to be born in an era where they had already invented sunscreen. I have learned to step over regrets and simply celebrate my treasured memories.

Tigger aka Fire Face

Armor

Aknight in shining armor may sound like the stuff of fairy tales but once upon a time, knighthood was serious business. Their armor was their only protection against the weapons of their enemies. The romantic knights of old, wore a very real armour of metal and chainmail, crafted to minimize the blows of the weapons of his or her enemies. Lances, long swords, maces, and arrows, were hard pressed to strike a mortal blow against the protection of the blacksmiths and armorers of the time.

But mother nature, through biology or action, has endowed some of our favorite creatures with armor of their own. A porcupine is a fine example. Armed with an array of quills, this critter rattles his sabers in warning and then slaps his tormenter with lances that not only penetrate the skin but unless removed, continue to dig deeper. Ouch!

How about the "slow loris," who covers himself with poison, or the bombardier beetle, who creates his own atomic bomb, to explode in the face of his attackers. The Iberian newt can expose its ribs through his skin, to create spikes as weapons and the horned toad can literally spit blood from its eyes, to deter weak stomached enemies.

Living in the southwest as I do, I must list a true hero... The opossum! Around the world almost a half-million people are bitten by snakes and more than twenty thousand of them die every year. People that is, not snakes. Opossums never have to worry about that, since they are immune to snake venom. They have a protein in their blood that binds to the toxins in snake venom and neutralizes it.

Scientists are looking into whether this protein could be used to treat human victims of snake bite. Thank you, opossums... Why not just use your "snake eyes" to avoid contact with these unpleasant rascals? The snakes, not the politicians!

Tigger

Bubbles

"**E**verything I like is either illegal, immoral or fattening…"
Hold it right their partner, I would like to offer an alternative view.

I must admit that this has been a most unusual time for us humans. We are quarantined away from family and friends. We have been ostracized from many of the familiar things that we know and love. Those of us of modest means, are trying to figure out how we will survive. The wealthy among us are discovering that you cannot buy off a virus and so, for now we are, as Don Maclean put it, "All in one place!" for who knows how long.

For all of my life, the best and the worst of it, seems that it has fallen to me to be the clown, the joker the family storyteller. I have been chosen the comedian. So, it was on a magic Easter morning, in 2018, that I brought the simplest of gifts, to share with our treasured friends. It was on the balcony of the Pacific's Edge Restaurant in Carmel California, full and happy after a fine breakfast, that I presented the Carmel Cruisers with their simple gifts.

The sea air smells like heaven, the sky is cobalt blue, the ocean is turbulent, and the kelp is dancing for us in its magnificence. Below us is what once was Kim Novak's beautiful beach home and the seals and otters are barking and singing a marvelous chorus, a beautiful morning!

So, what are we doing? We are all playing with a small plastic bottle and a wand. Eighteen adults, along with our offspring are hanging over the balcony and blowing bubbles into the wind and out toward the great Pacific. What a simple joy for each of us. You do not need Highway One or the Pacific Ocean to play a bit.

Bubbles! Won't you join us! Four bottles of joy for $13.38, from Amazon. Send me a photo please!

Tigger

Mom

In my most recent book, "Sunlight and Shadows," I took a turn at writing a bit about my family. Readers enjoyed it! The main comment was, "I learned more about you and yours in my first reading of your new book, than I ever learned hearing you speak on stage for twenty years. Cool...

I'm never sure when or what time of year you will be reading these Chronicles, but I am composing this one during the week of Saint Patrick's Day. Until recently, I had never known who my father was, but Irish seems to be a major genetic component of my DNA, (England, Scotland, Wales). That being said, there is little wonder that I have such a powerful, joyous connection to things and people of the emerald isle.

Our mother had a beautiful voice. Although she sang everything from standards to Hawaiian melodies, she was a wonder at children's songs, stories, and lullabies. So, it is at this time of year, that each morning as I start up my mountain, there is a certain tune on my lips and in my heart. *"Too-Ra-Loo-Ra-Loo-Ral-Too Ra-Loo-Ra-Li (That's an Irish Lullaby.)"*

"Over in Killarney, many years ago, me mither sang a song to me in tones so sweet and low. Just a simple little ditty in her good ould Irish way, and I'd give the world to have her sing that

song to me this day..."

Often as a child my health was challenged and so, on many of my struggling-to-breathe oxygen-starved nights, I was truly comforted and sung to sleep by my mother's sweet and lilting voice. *"Too-Ra-Loo-Ra-Loo-Ral..."* I truly hadn't thought of it until just now but perhaps my mom was sending a message regarding the identity of me real father when she would croon this simple but beautiful tune.

Won't you hum it with me now?

O'Tigger

Brilliant!

The richly decorated hotel lobby was wall to wall with sharp looking individuals, laughing, conversing, and sipping their coffee. There was no doubt, from their appearance and demeanor, that they were the best of the best. Their voices revealed the excitement and anticipation felt for the meetings to come. From all over the world, six hundred of the best business partners a company could hope to find, had joined us. These were our distributors and they had travelled around the globe to share in our discoveries, creations and to confirm their commitment to carry our products into the beauty salons in their territories. They were masters of demonstrating our science and inviting their fine salons to carry, display and recommend our unique professional formulations. Wow!

My good fortune, as senior vice president of the company, was to welcome our international guests, both in the lobby, socially and then from the stage, as keynote speaker. What an exhilarating experience, to stand before an audience in which the people seated before me, spoke a collected twenty-seven different languages.

Once on stage, I offered a heartfelt welcome to our dignitaries and in their enthusiastic response, I heard one excited guest yell, "Brilliant!" At the time of this convention, I had been speaking in public and on stage, for better than fifty years and I had never, in all of those years, heard that loud, clear declaration of support: "Brilliant!" Much intrigued, I waited till the first coffee break and then began the search for the young bloke that I had observed crying out in support.

When we finally connected, he explained that the expression he used was a common one in South Africa. It was the equivalent of our "Hooray!" I offered to trade epithets and he just replied, "Use it Tigger!"

Brilliant!

Asclepius

That's what I said too! Who, and how do you pronounce that? "Uh-sklee-pee-us!" He is the deity associated with healing and medicinal arts in Greek mythology. He is the son of Apollo, the physician. He became so proficient in healing that he surpassed his father and was believed to be able to evade death and bring others back from the brink of death and beyond. I tried to get in for an appointment, don't bother... He's booked solid!

This mythological adventure began on a recent morning walk, as I finished my mountain climb and headed down into our neighborhood. I love this part, because there is nothing like a few good howdies along the way, to brighten your journey. On the corner of our street, where the road turns down to head past the golf course and on into the city, I spied a vine, about the circumference of your finger, twisted around a wrought iron fence rod. The yard was under some serious landscaping and so where once there grew a large shrub from earth to sky, now only the dead vines themselves remained, wrapped tightly around the fencing, and clinging like a forlorn lover.

As I paused to rest and stare at this intriguing bit of nature's artwork, I realized that it looked very familiar. Wherever medicine is practiced, there is often a sign bearing an insignia which includes a staff with a serpent wrapped around it. It is known as the true symbol of medicine, The Staff of "Asclepius." I admire my doctors.

Why a snake, I wondered? Turns out that in Greek mythology, snakes were considered sacred. The creature that we so often see, wrapped around the rod, may symbolize rejuvenation, because snakes shed their skin, or it could simply represent the healing of snakebites. In any case, I was surprised and happy to have found this excellent image of the healing arts and wondered if the landscapers had even noticed the logo on the fence?

Curious Tigger

Click

Years ago, I read the book, "Clicking," by Faith Popcorn. It was a good read and a pop best seller. I also had the pleasure of sharing the children's story "Chicken Clicking," by Jean Willis. These bits of literary wonder were the virtual birthplace of this Desert Wind. All I needed was to click! Read on...

We have a wonderful young friend who came to us when his mom married one of our sons. His name is Bobby, and he and his brother and sister are human treasures. I write about Bobby not to exclude his siblings but because he communicates with us on a regular basis. We pretty much celebrate everything about him. His courage definitely tops the list. He is an English Coach, residing in Hokkaido, Japan and he has been kind enough to post a newsletter for family and friends. We have just enjoyed number eight in the series. He clicked and the news sent. I clicked and it opened up.

Imagine, as I sit comfortably at my desk, in Nevada, I am reading and digesting the adventures of a young man, occurring more than five-thousand miles away. He is studying, teaching, eating, sleeping, caring for his health, and all the while enlightening his young students. He is doing all of this, halfway around the world. He is teaching English while he is learning Japanese. He is by his own choice, learning a whole new culture, a brand-new landscape, along with strange foods, and customs . We are so proud of him. All of this, shared as a gift of technology. Click!

My youngest son and I are working on a children's book, about the royal cranes of Hokkaido, so with Bobby's permission, I forwarded a rough draft of our manuscript. He was kind enough to read it and share his positive response. Click!

No matter how divisive and distant our world can seem, a closer union, a richer relationship, is truly one click away.

Tigger

Evening Primrose

How many wonderful stories have been told and sung about the ragged, starving girl, discovered on the wrong side of the tracks, only later to be revealed as royalty. Cinderella, Mulan, and the beautiful Rose in Spanish Harlem... These wonderful fairy tales are crafted from the brilliant, creative minds of fine authors who have never given away their childlike vision. Through vivid images, color, and storytelling, they place in our minds, the possibility of clearing away the dust, dirt, poverty, starvation and often cruelty, to becoming the royalty that can be our birthright.

Our home is in the Mojave Desert. Compared to Santa Barbara or Carmel, California, both places in which I have lived, many might view our current residence as a garden ghetto. One mountain range away from the Pacific Ocean, it is cold in winter, windy in spring and hot as hades in the summertime. It is dry and dusty. This would seem to be a perfect setting from which to seek and find a potential fairytale princess. Surprise!

Following the guidance of our fearless leaders, we have waited patiently for approval to visit friends and neighbors for a barbecue. Now, vaccinated and cleared for just such a visit, we were sitting in the wonderful patio of our long- time pals. As our conversation wandered into the settling darkness, I spotted, in the corner of their yard, a group of what appeared to be soft-pink flowers bobbing in the strong desert breeze. I whipped out my trusty iPhone camera and set about trying to capture these bobbing pink treasures. As I began snapping these shy wonders, my neighbor saw me in action and exclaimed, "those are just weeds you know!"

We are not born in palaces and into royalty and wealth. If we are "fairytale" fortunate, we will be carried on the Desert Wind, to land in the yard of a marvelous gardener like our friend Steve, who with a few drops of water, patience, and some desert sun, can turn weeds into wonders.

Tigger

Honeysuckle

Each year when the Masters Golf Tourney rolls around, my mind drifts south. Our neighbors are avid golfers and have witnessed the pageant that is Augusta, many times. Though I am a Southern California boy by birth, my mind, like my travels, has given me the opportunity to see, smell and taste a whole world of floral wonders. As Azaleas are the theme and centerpiece of the Masters, Honeysuckle is a blessing to our desert.

At Thanksgiving time in the southwest, almost every yard features a rich green bush that displays a burst of lovely red flowers. On my daily wanderings I don't have to wait long to witness the hummingbird battles that are fought over this sweet, fragrant, and colorful vine. It is a coral honeysuckle, and whether here in Nevada or in the Peach State, we love our sweet blossoms.

A thing of beauty, coral honeysuckle was revered for its medicinal purposes. The leaves were chewed and the resulting mush, placed on a bee sting, eased the pain. The leaves were even dried and smoked as an aid to asthma. Self sufficient and drought resistant, it is the perfect plant for the desert of our monastery.

Honeysuckle dances in my memory, for as small boy I recall playing around the beautiful white blossoms in our yard, to find myself entranced by the honey-like fragrance of these flowers.

I discovered that by pulling out the tiny little stamens of these delicate flowers, I could, like my hummingbird friends, savor the actual honey that was hidden within.

Imagine the surprise that my doubting little sister experienced, when she first took a chance and touched her tongue to the amber liquid on that tiny thread. Don't take my word for it. Click it up on Youtube and watch it being done. You are so "sweet" to share my stories...

Tigger

Brothers!

My older brother, of whom I have often written, was indeed my hero. As a lad, seven years my senior, it seemed that he was always into some adventure just beyond my boundaries. His willingness to expose me to such things, became a tantalizing and formative influence in my life. From driving his own car, to shooting off fireworks and firearms, he and his friends were the stars of my life's movie and quite an inspiration.

He would often leave things out in his room, no doubt in the hope that I would "discover," them. My favorite was literature. So it was that I came to read such classics as "Richard Halliburton's "Travel's," "On the Beach" by Nevil Shute, "The Moon is Down," by John Steinbeck, and many more. He was an earnest student and a serious chap, strange that it is the funny stuff that stuck with me over all of these decades. Behind his closed bedroom door, all it took was his laughter to get me wondering what he was thinking, doing, or reading, in that inner sanctum of his.

After one evening of being tantalized by his gales of laughter, when at last his door popped open, a curious kid brother couldn't wait to beg for entry and to be enlightened. It was a paperback that had inspired his mirth. Laying on his bed, was a cartoon book by the great artist and writer, Walt Kelly. "The Pogo Stepmother Goose" was the story, and the opening line was all it took. On the first page, as Pogo, Walt's most famous character, comes upon Mother Goose, played by Albert Alligator, he observed that "she looked like she had swallowed a bandicoot!" Today as my brother and I sip a cocktail and exchange quotes from Walt Kelly's many stories, I realize that I still love to say the word "bandicoot..." Just for the fun of it.

As a mesmerized seven-year-old, I could not have foreseen that one day, many years hence, I would be invited to tour Australia, at which time I would visit Steve Irwin's Australia Zoo and be introduced to a real live bandicoot.

Rest in Peace my beloved Brother AKA Buddy
Tigger

Key Largo

Beneath a crisp blue autumn sky, the breeze created a welcome swirl of colorful leaves along Peachtree Street. While on the inside, the southern beau's and belles were lining up for some cheering, screaming, and education. For the quarter of a century that we presented our inspiration and business Challenges around the world, there was never an opening day that we were not thrilled, excited, and honored to be there. Preparing to open the doors of the beautiful Hyatt Ballroom in Atlanta, we were filled with memories of last night's dinner on Pittypats Porch and our runaway carriage ride (honest and true) we were all geared up for an exciting seminar.

I reminded our team that a presentation in Atlanta was like no other. Unlike other cities with their often "show-me" attitudes, southern folk made the show a wonder with their grace, courtesy, manners, and participation.

With our newest team member in hand, we turned on the entry music, opened the great doors and welcomed five hundred of the south's greatest professional hairdressers and salon owners. The excitement was palpable!

As we walked along the front row of the audience, offering our welcome by shaking hands and sharing a hug for old friends and fans, we were reveling in sweet southern drawl, when a perfectly dressed and coiffured bo-peep came straight up to us and introduced herself. "Howdy, y'all, we are sure blest that you are here..." The music surrounded us and filled the room. Bertie Higgins was singing, "We had it all, just like Bogie and Bacall." As we stood enchanted by this gone with wind lassie, she leaned forward and whispered: "You aren't going to believe this... But I am the Key Largo girl." With her honeysuckle voice, southern charm, grace, and exquisite stature, we knew for sure that she was the lady for whom the song was written and performed.

And sailing away to Key Largo
Tigger

Marv (Part One)

On a warm, sunny afternoon, in a lavish Las Vegas ballroom, I was giving a presentation for the "Intercoiffure" national fall atelier. This is the American Beauty Industry's most prestigious professional association. To be chosen to share the stage in front of these great and successful artisans is truly and honor.

Gathered together, these world class salon owners, stylists, and makeup artists had come to learn, share, to see and be seen. For me it was a red-carpet adventure. I finished my presentation and was pleased to feel the enthusiasm that came from the audience.

He sat on the aisle, in the very last row. This position gave me a fine view of his wide, friendly face and a clear shot at his broad shoulders and jolly smile. He wore what appeared to me to be a Cricketeer gentlemen's sport jacket of forest green, with a perfectly knotted wool tie and at his feet rested his fine leather briefcase. This was man of class.

For those of us that speak and perform in public, there is often a face in the audience that appears to enjoy our labors a bit more than the others. They listen more deeply, respond more thoroughly, laugh more genuinely, and applaud more enthusiastically. This was that man, and I couldn't wait till the coffee break to head out to greet him. His friendly handshake was the beginning of a lifelong friendship. He was a scout master and a mountain man... So was I. He loved telling stories and laughing...So did I. In the days and years that followed our meeting, we did classes together. We celebrated his family's receipt of their star on the Hollywood Boulevard, and he very kindly showed me how makeup could be applied to create a smooth appearance in the *face* of skin cancer. Imagine my shock when watching these Academy Awards, that I saw his name in Memoriam..." I will miss you Marv Westmore. (More to come...)

Tigger

Marv (Part Two)

The wound was ghastly! A knife fight was my best guess. As the class walked past, one by one, examining the gash on the man's arm, it was astounding to think that we were observing some rare movie magic. Under the watchful eye of the studio's founder, Marv Westmore, we had been invited to watch a makeup master presenting a special effects workshop, at the Westmore Academy, in Burbank, CA. The make-up was so realistic that one of our class members asked, "How soon will those stiches come out?"

Marvin (Marv) Westmore, was the son of Monte Westmore and a part of the famed Westmore's of Hollywood. Marv was more than a makeup artist. He was a teacher, a mentor, and an innovator, who never lost his love and passion for the artistry of makeup. You know him through his incredible collection of work, Murder She Wrote, Lanky, The Rat Pack, Blade Runner, Escape and Vegas Vacation, where Marv took time for lunch with us, back in his trailer, and showed me how makeup, properly applied, could make skin cancer disappear on the screen.

He was a world-class master of eye makeup! You could never sit in a Westmore class, for they were standing room only. One was truly spellbound, as he took the most difficult eyebrow techniques and turned every actress and every model, into a glamour queen.

He was so knowledgeable and yet gentle in his manner, that he put both housewives and Hollywood stars at ease, the moment he set his hand on client's shoulder.

Together we made movies and videos and laughed until we cried. I wish that every speaker, like myself, could find that one member of the audience and realize that the real stars are not the ones on stage. As Marv always said to me in parting, See you down the trail, Mountain Man!

Tigger

The Porch

I recently overheard an architect discussing some new homes he was building nearby. The potential buyers had just asked him about the porch that seemed to be missing from the blueprint. His answer, "a porch is just a waste of space!"

For me, the porch was the place that dad departed each morning for work and returned every evening. This enchanted little piece of real estate was my pirate ship, my fortress, a place for real-life wartime departures and arrivals. It was the spot where lemonade, iced tea, homemade ice cream and sandwiches always tasted the absolute best. Back in the day a porch was a magic carpet and a time-machine. Fortunately, the builders who constructed our little today home here in the monastery, included that wonderful appurtenance known as a porch.

Our porch guests have included quail, huge lizards, chipmunks, a five-foot-long red racer snake, tarantulas, scorpions, and a desert tortoise, named Tuesday, (because that was the day she arrived.) Add to these, some treasured neighbors and most recently a beautiful southwestern speckled rattlesnake, curled up, asleep, outside our front door. Now I know that this kind of information can be startling, and I can hear a few of you mumbling, "Well, we're not going to the Cox's and that's it!"

First let me reassure you that I thoroughly checked out this beautiful reptile. He was obviously homeless, because he had slept on our porch all curled up and cozy. He looked as if he had just shed his skin, as he was smooth and brightly colored. These rascals eat rats and mice, and he was wearing his pest exterminator uniform. He had his I.D. He frightened our neighbors, so I decided to send him on his way. I did my best to handcuff him. Have you ever tried to handcuff a snake? We finally got him ready, packed his little bag, whipped up a lunch and sent him off to camp itchy-ouchy. He seemed excited.

Tigger

Fire

Fire! It warms our homes, cooks our food, and provides dancing shadows on the walls of our winter homes. On the other side, the Desert Wind has its own moods and seasons. From her summer blast furnace at one-hundred-ten degrees, to the winter's chinook, this column's namesake is a wonder.

Today as I head home from the mountain, she is showing her winter-side. It is below freezing; twenty knots, and it cuts through my down jacket like a hunting knife. This morning it sends a chill through my garments and chills me to the bone. I am looking forward to stepping out of the wind, into my living room and a blessed chance to warm myself before the fire.

Since I was a child, every home in which I lived, was blessed with a fireplace. It was more than just warmth. It was a gathering place for our family and friends on a cold winter's night. Fires don't just start by themselves, either outdoors or indoors. There is an art to fire-craft that takes teaching, training, and experience. In elementary school I had the pleasure of reading the famous short story, "To Build a Fire," in which an inept woodsman perished for failing to start and maintain a fire in the snow. In Junior High I was enchanted reading Jack London's bestselling novel "Call of the Wild." It is about Buck, a domestic dog living near my boyhood home in the Santa Clara Valley. He is dognapped and sold into the goldrush world of the Klondike. Now I recall the passage where Buck has flashbacks of a time shared with a cave man, more animal than human.

Each time I find myself warming my bones before a blazing fire, I realize that I am also warming the prehistoric memories of lifetimes long gone by. Whether your home is built with a fireplace or not, you can share this adventure in literature, mind, and spirit. S'mores?

Tigger

Gear

It all sounded so grand in the beginning; a few days away from the city, out in the fresh air, communing with wild critters, and a chance to change my perspective. Then you curled up for your first night on the ground in the wilderness and you never wanted to hear the word *camping* again! You've been there... The *best* night or the *worst* night of your life!

Many of my readers took the time to respond to my recent series of our adventures at the "The Trestle." We were camping in the desert and some of you have decided not to come along! I love to hear from you and get your slant on things. You shared how cold and uncomfortable you had been on your outdoor sleepovers. Sorry 'bout that. As a scout master, which I enjoyed, I realized that the boys under my leadership deserved a chance to venture out away from humankind and to live, although briefly, in the wild. I decided that I was going to make certain that these fine lads, though not pampered, had the very best opportunity to enjoy the journey to the fullest.

On my checklist was, warmth, plenty of fresh water, simple but good food and the opportunity to contribute to camp life. I loved to replace their common fears with excitement and their city experience, with a chance to rough it for a few days. After my first boyhood cold night in the mountains, I decided to figure out how to sleep warm, dry, and cozy and to make a joy out of roughing it. In the end it all Came down to gear.

Clothing came first. Layers mean comfort at a wide range of temperatures. Plenty to stay warm with the setting sun and easily removed to make a noon hike just right. What you sleep on and in, is forever the main complaint. "I don't ever want to sleep on the ground!" you say. Why would you? A self- inflating sleep pad and a warm, easy to care for sleeping bag will do it. I've had the joy of camping, from the deserts of Arizona to the mountains of Alaska, and I can't wait to go again... You coming?

Tigger

Is That Your Kite?

It all started a day earlier, when my sons and I were discussing the fact that we had not built and flown one of our giant homemade kites in a while. We all agreed that it was time and Friday afternoon would be the launch. On the cool, windy Thursday before, we gathered in our den and bent over the coffee table to our work.

We started the evening with a cup of hot Dr. Pepper with lemon wedges from our tree. It seemed that it was all the juice we needed to create our masterpiece. Fine balsa wood struts, kite string, a package of rainbow-colored tissue paper, a roll of last Christmas' scotch tape, lots of laughter and we were set. By the time we finalized our construction and parted company, we were set and excited for tomorrow's launch.

Now there are many different locations from which we had turned loose our treasure, but today, with chicken marinating in the cooler, fresh local greens and veggies for our salad and Hawaiian bread, the only place that made sense was Goleta Beach. We flew our beautiful, sturdy kites into the wild blue yonder and so we tethered the guide string to about a mile of ninety-pound test fishing line on a handsome fine pole and a deep-sea reel, that could accommodate that much heavy mono.

Once on the beach and no time wasted, we turned her into the wind and began to pay out the line. Oh, my how she danced! We all took a turn and by the time it came back to me, the line was out. "Is that your kite?" came the stern, deep voice. I looked down at the pole and reel in my hands, the line stretching out into the blue, turned to the sheriff, and replied. "Yep..." As the FAA and two other unmarked cars pulled up, I asked: "Is anything wrong officer?" Turns out our rainbow beauty was one mile out and directly in the incoming flight path of the Santa Barbara Airport.

Ticked off pilots...
Roo (Not going to give my real name!)

On the Nose

Outside our bedroom window the moon is rising over Doug's Mountain. All but the skyline is pitch black. The house is silent, save for a distant poorwill singing his last lullaby. In our darkened bedroom I feel what I imagine to be a reindeer, leap from the floor, to land directly on my legs. No need to check the clock, it is five A.M. How do I know this? Because our alarm cat is never wrong!

I am at my desk working on my newest book. Suddenly, the sweetest little sleepy, furry face, appears around the corner of our hallway. I don't need to look up. I know that it is twelve noon sharp! How does she know this?

Wrapping up my day's labors, I see a slow-moving feature moseying across our living room carpet and heading for my office. Without a second thought, I know that it is five P.M. How is this possible?

I have often wondered if this uncanny ability to know the time of day is unique to our kitty-cat? While scientists tell us that cats can't tell time from a clock (as far as we know,) they do have a general sense of time. It is said that they keep track of when things usually happen and know full well if we are not sticking to their mealtimes. Over-sleeping is not acceptable! Cats, they reveal, are crepuscular, meaning that they are primarily active around dawn and dusk, except for the occasional midnight hockey game under our bed.

The same way that we get hungry around lunchtime and know it's been a few hours since breakfast, cats will judge how long it's been since their last meal and that's how they know to tell us that their meal is overdue... Three Oclock, our cat, doesn't arouse me to make sure that I finish this Desert Wind, she wakes me because she knows that I will reward her behavior with plenty of head scratches and snuggles. See? One thing we know for sure, she is right twice a day. Tis written all over her face.

Tigger-Time
ThreeOclockOnTheNose.com

Sing

Unless it is one-hundred-ten degrees or the smoke from wild- fires fills the air, I pass him nearly every day. Whether dawn or dusk, like a character on his way to OZ, he comes heading my way swinging his arms vigorously, walking with pride and go figure, he is singing!

I love inspiration and, on any day, particularly pandemic days, I am on alert for some. So, a Tin Man, a Cowardly Lion, a happy fellow hiker, or a pal from Texas, is bound to catch my attention.

Recently our wonderful friends, Wayne, and Debby, from the Lone Star State, sent me a text. It was just a simple southern, "Howdy," but it seemed to shine a little brighter than all of the others arriving on my smart phone that day. Both of these two lifelong friends had written to share that they were preparing to sing online with their church choir. Not only did they share their *glee,* pun is absolutely intended, but they also *noted,* enough with the puns, the name and page of the hymn they had prepared for Sunday go meetin'.

I am a singer too. It brings me joy climbing the Rockies, surfing the pacific, patrolling Fort Lauderdale, by the sea, or cruising highway 101, you will definitely find me singing.

A pandemic is a tough time for all. The door seems closed on so many things that once brought a smile, gave us reason to laugh and brought joy to our lives. Why not just make a little music for ourselves and then, like my neighbor, on his way to meet the Wizard, share it with others. You say, "I couldn't do that! I can't sing a note." One morning I got close enough to my neighbor to say, " I sure do enjoy your singing."

His response, "Oh, I couldn't carry a tune in a bushel basket!" I replied, "Please don't tell yourself, it could ruin a great day for both of us!"

Tigger

Tables

There is something about tables that I find fascinating. I love the social aspect of simply dining, whether it be a casual family-only meal or a Thanksgiving Feast before the fire at the great table in the ranch dining room at Palo Alto, California. As an executive-inspirational-trainer, I have produced and presided over many a table meeting of dignitaries, from big time to regular folks, from performers to presidents. There is always an intriguing purpose for pulling oneself, belly up to a table, be it dining or doing business.

During the Dunhill Record days of Three Dog Night, Steppenwolf, and the Mamas and Papas, it was my pleasure to hang out with this talented, crazy, and creative group of writers, producers, and performers. Among my favorites was Richard Harris. He was a fine actor and a wild one. I am a fan of Arthurian literature and that is how I end up each year, watching my friend's portrayal of King Arthur, in the film version of Camelot. To me the idea of a round table with all of its intent and wonder, is a great concept.

I also love "Timetables" from railroads around America, the great "Stone Table," from the marvelous C.S. Lewis book, "The Lion the Witch and the Wardrobe," and then there is one other.

Recently I have had the great joy of sharing cocktails and

conversation around the great "Round Glass Table," in Lancaster, Pennsylvania. Our long-time friend and colleague Paula has been courageous enough to share with us that she has been diagnosed with cancer. She and her man Jack have been kind enough to bring us together, at her table, on many occasions, to share great laughter, painful tears and the blessings of our life and living.

Paula's friends make the most wonderful use of their time at the table, sharing their heroic past and planning a brilliant future. I can think of no higher purpose for the use of a round table than this.

Tigger, or as Jimmy Webb composed for Richard Harris, A Tramp Shining!

Moments

There are so many wonderful moments in a lifetime. There are before's, and during's and after's. A three act wonder for us in our loge seats! I'm not good at math but I imagine the equation might look something like this: Before+During+After=Life! And for me, life, for all of its ups and downs=Joy!

Winnie The Pooh is a *before kind* of bear who likes the moment before he first tastes the honey. "Well," said Pooh, "what I like best," and then he had to stop and think. Because although Eating Honey was a very good thing to do, there was a moment just before you began to eat it, which was better than when you were, but he didn't' know what it was called.

Robin Hood is a *now* kind of outlaw who likes the moment that he is in as he, on his stump in Sherwood Forest, reminds his Merrie Men that: "Faint hearts Never Won Fair Ladies!"

Tom Jones is a handsome *after* kind of romantic, who savors the memory: "I'll sing you to sleep, after the lovin'..."

For me, it is all of the above, like the moment when I hear distant thunder and catch the first whiff of moisture in the desert air. Then the first sound of raindrops bringing the reward for our patience, faith, and prayers. And finally, the glory after the rain when our world has been painted with raindrops and He is reminding us how blest we are to have noses.

Anticipation, fascination and at last celebration! I am touched by the fact that the folks with whom we share these glories, either large or small, are passing from this world and in doing so take with them our ability to share.

Hard to imagine that many in the newest generation are never given the opportunity or the inspiration to stop to enjoy them...

Lucky Tigger

The Club

George is the coolest guy. He is a pickle-baller with a great smile and a terrific friendly demeanor. So, when I saw him heading down the street toward me, I was a happy man. Instead of turning up the hill to my mountain, I crossed over and awaited his arrival.

After our courteous but six-foot distant greeting he said, "We sure miss you guys!" Not sure who he meant, I asked for clarification, and he pointed out that he was referring to our "Variety Club." He went on to explain how much the community loved our annual spring show and how sad they were when Covid 19 closed the curtains on our 2020 event.

Now, there we were, standing in the street together, eight months into the year and well past the performance dates of our production and George was telling us how important we were to our community. I write all this because there are a half-a-hundred of us who truly put our hearts and souls into this event, and I wanted every one of them to know they were remembered and to feel the recognition and importance of their talents and labors.

For our cast and crew, it had been a heartbreak for us to announce the pandemic postponement of our production. Singers, dancers, comedians, magicians, and all of the stagehands it takes to keep the show on track, had created and begun rehearsing their special part in our show. It takes hours and weeks to prep for such a performance and this cancellation took the wind out of our sails. We have a fine auditorium in which we present our programs and each of our three annual performances is pretty well sold out.

I want to say that we, as a part of the team, are honored to be remembered and ready to get on with the show the moment Covid packs up and moves on!

Tigger

The Tree

P iglet's house is in a large old oak, in the heart of what Christopher Robin came to know as the Hundred Acre Wood. Owl's house was also in one of the taller trees in the middle of that magical place. As you recall, in *Winnie the Pooh and the bustery day*, owl's house was blown down. After this, Piglet, in a very noble act, decided to give his own house to Owl and go to live with Pooh for the time being. Inspired to share this now, because so many residents in the western United States are suffering through horrendous brush fires and living in great peril and fear of the loss of their homes and property. Once, long ago a huge brush fire raced through the canyon where we lived in Santa Barbara, and we were faced with the same prospect of returning home to find everything gone.

As you are aware, trees provide an incredible array of gifts to those who live in and around them. Acting as the lungs of the earth, they improve air quality by capturing pollution in their leaves and producing Oxygen through photosynthesis. They are champions of water conservation by catching the few precious drops of moisture that fall in our parched desert. Their roots hold soil in place. One hundred mature trees can intercept about one-hundred-thousand gallons of rainfall each year. Trees soften the climate, provide wildlife habitat, and to a hiker like me... cast a cooling shade. Trees improve our health by reducing stress and imparting a sense of wellbeing. It is a fact that hospital patients with a window looking out on trees, recover faster.

In a time like this, with drought across the land, trees can begin to die and become a danger to the residence and the humans below. Weakened by wind and weather, drought, disease, and insects, these trees succumb to the pressure and fall. As these old beauties become cracked and brittle, we must ready ourselves for the final goodbye. Such is the case with our neighbor's tall and graceful friend.

A thankful Tigger

Sleeping Out

It was a warm Friday afternoon in the beautiful Santa Barbara foothills. Late summer seemed to bring out the best in us and our surroundings. The bright blue pacific, sparkling in the distance, was sending its richest fragrance up Coyote Canyon and the eucalyptus trees were responding with their healing perfume. As our wonderful kids arrived home, one by one, we gathered in the kitchen for a snack. A Cox tradition was to debrief before we disband and so it was that we stopped to chat. I inquired and listened completely to each of their school reports and then I released the surprise. "How about it" I asked? As I watched my children's eyes light up, I knew that I had hit on the right approach. "How would you like to sleep out tonight?"

It wasn't like it was the first time we had camped out, but our summer had been quite busy and therefore we were itching to feel the earth and watch the stars. I did not happen to mention that tonight was the peak of the Perseids Meteor Shower and there was a very good chance the dark rich coastal night sky would provide a perfect velvet background for our celestial adventure.

One of my great joys as a presenter has been to share our family adventures with my audiences. I recall one fine group in New York, who when I suggested a sleep out, argued that there was no way to get out of the city, setup camp, spend a night or two in the woods, break down the gear and then return to their urban residence. I responded that I had not suggested a journey but instead, had invited my kids to sleep out in our own back yard!

Sharp New Yorkers laughed aloud and exclaimed that they didn't have a back yard. It was then that I played my ace card. When I was young and very broke, I had rented a tiny apartment with a sliding glass door looking out towards downtown. I simply pulled my sleeping bag up to that doorway and slept looking up through the screen onto the night sky. And guess what? no mosquitos. Wherever we find ourselves we can create an adventure.

"Camp Itchy-Ouchy" awaits... Tigger

Turquoise

She danced into the afternoon sunlight... darting this way and that. This beautiful dragonfly *(Taniil' ai in Navajo)* had returned like an old friend, to remind me of the history and joy of my favorite gemstone. It was as if ten-thousand-years of history, medicine and magic had flown back into my life. If this winged gemstone means this much to me, a twenty-first century Anglo, imagine what it means to the Native and Aboriginal peoples who found it and turned it into a significant part of their art and spiritual culture. Scientists and geologists refer to it as *Hydrated phosphate of copper and aluminum.* We simply call it Turquoise.

Long after the ancient Egyptians entombed their pharos with turquoise studded jewelry and Persians had come to associate the glory of victory and virtue of holiness with this gem, the story of this precious stone became a part of our Native American history.

In the beginning Atsidi Sani, the Navajo artisan learned from the Mexican silversmiths, to craft pieces of artwork that held viewers spell bound. Rings, bracelets, cuffs, figurines and beautiful conchos, adorned tribal members and fanciers alike. In Beverly Hills they refer to this stone as a portal to positive energy. Whether in the flickering light of a campfire, at a red-carpet fashion show or around the negotiating table in Washington, DC, the rich, blue-green hues of this beautiful stone spoke to friend and foe alike, of strength, skill, and invincibility.

Many generations of believers have discovered that this gem holds many gifts of the spirit. The artisans of the southwest brought to life the true beauty of these stone pieces, both large and small. Their stunning jewelry caught the eye of traders and merchants who took the artwork across America, to Central and South America and around the world. Although I love every precious piece of my Native American artwork, I treasure my turquoise above all.

Lucky Tigger

Jazz

My dear friend was once again pouring his heart and soul into that sweet saxophone of his. I couldn't wait to see and hear the great Charles Lloyd making that timeless connection. When I announced this to some friends of mine, one of them exclaimed, "Jazz... You kidding me? I just don't get it!" Some of the funniest stand-up routines have been aimed at that wonderful form of music and those of us who play and celebrate it.

Jazz: Let's start with the fact that you love something that doesn't work for me. Salad dressing for example. While you pour out that flavorful elixir onto your salad, I am realizing one swig out of that bottle would send me to the hospital. I am allergic to vinegar. That's food jazz!

Haven't you ever had a friend or colleague say, "I just don't get that guy or gal!" that's people jazz! Writing about cowboys, Willy Nelson said, "He ain't wrong he's just different and his pride won't let him do things to make you think he's right!" That's cowboy jazz! We have a beloved friend who can't abide avocados and artichokes... That's guacamole jazz!

From the Lighthouse Cafe, in Hermosa Beach, California where I first met Chet Baker, to the Blackhawk, in the tenderloin of San Francisco, where my dad took me at age fourteen to see the

Dave Brubeck Quartet, to the Balboa Pavilion in Newport Beach, California, where I first discovered Stan Kenton, to the beautiful trees above the Monterey Fairgrounds and the Jazz Festival that gave us Charles Lloyd...I love jazz.

One of the things our mom left with us is the joy found in our differences. Dissonance, tight harmony, solos by fours, or as Edward Greig wrote, Strange Music! Don't go into space without it!

Tigger

Tolstoy

How I love his writing. *War and Peace, Anna Karenina,* and *The Cossacks,* are top shelf in my literary world. I remember sharing the heart-warming story of *Martin the Cobbler* with my children as a Christmas tradition. Considered to be one of the greatest authors of all time, Tolstoy is worthy of our celebration. Today however, it is another that I would share, as a focus of this Desert Wind. "Tolstoy," the great bull elephant of Africa.

At one time, in Kenya, the sight of a giant bull elephant, or "tusker" as they are known, was a frequent if not common site on the savannah. These gigantic, gentle, intelligent creatures, standing thirteen feet tall and weighing eleven tons, are the images that most frequently come to mind when we think of Africa and its wonderful wildlife. On either side of their broad, handsome faces, is a tusk weighing about one-hundred pounds. This ivory is the glory of these beautiful beasts. Sadly though, it is also the reason for their disappearance.

Elephants are social creatures and are Masters of Communication. They love to talk to each other and do so by vocalizing a wide range of calls and sounds. From the trumpeting that we know in the movies, to the less audible rumbles of reassurance, science has identified at least seventy different calls. The latest research reveals that they also reach out with a series of infrasound's, inaudible to the human ear, that the herd can hear up to fourteen miles away. Recent studies have revealed pachyderms may also be able to communicate with seismic waves that travel through the ground and are picked up through their feet.

The word "elephant" is actually Latin for huge arch and the name fits, as elephants are the largest living land mammals in the world. Where once these gentle giants roamed across the whole of Africa, they are now limited to conservation areas and the savannah. Poachers slaughter around thirty-five thousand "tuskers" each year.

We Roam Together,
Tolstoy and Tigger

Wilson

In the parking lot outside the school where our kids spent their mornings, you would see our big, blue Cadillac, idling and ready for the adventure. With Aloha Racks locked down on the roof and surf boards at the ready, we were California Surf Style for sure. Once the bell rang, out the door and across the striped pavement came the excited young Cox's, juggling their books and running toward our version of the California dream.

Depending on the swell and the weather, we would head straight for Taco Bell, our bag of burritos and a tray of Cokes. Next stop... College Point and an afternoon of riding waves. Our brood started young, around six-years-old, and the sound of that scream echoing across the water, was a rite of passage, as they successfully caught their first wave. Paddling into the green, cold salt water, rising onto their waxed sticks, and navigating their way through the kelp covered rocks, this was as good as it gets. Every moment was an endless summer for this dad.

One misty, warm pacific afternoon as I was loading our boards, I noticed that the racks we were using were starting to cut into the rails on the roof of the blue beauty, so I made a quick decision and a slight detour. For most of this summer, on my route to and from school, I had seen an old Volkswagen Bug with a hand drawn "For Sale" sign in the window. Until this afternoon, it had never crossed my mind that this was a classic surf buggy, just waiting for a handful of beach rats to spiff that baby up and climb aboard. Five-hundred bucks did it and the pink slip was mine.

I will never forget the look on our kid's faces, as they scanned the parking lot searching for the "Blue Bird." Finally, they spotted me at the wheel of this righteous ride. Next stop, the beach, where we sat in the sand to hold council and choose a name: *"Wilson!"* was the name we chose.

On the way home Brian and his brothers were singing *"Let's Go Surfing Now..."* it was obvious how and why Wilson got his name.

Tigger

Ice Cream

"**E**verything I like is either illegal, immoral or fattening..." Hold it right their partner, I would like to respectfully disagree.

I must admit that this has been a most unusual time for us humans. We are quarantined away from family and friends. We have been ostracized from many of the familiar things that we know and love. Those with modest means are trying to figure out how we will survive. The wealthy among us are discovering that you cannot buy off a virus and so for now, we are as Don Maclean put it in his song, American Pie, "all in one place:" and not having much fun!

What we need is something to bring back the fun; something that the corona cops can't take away from us...I've got the answer! Ice Cream.

For me, the ice cream adventure began a long time ago on the back porch of our farmhouse in Pasadena California, where we were churning homemade ice cream. As a little farm hand (5 years old) I'm sure that I could have cared less what flavor we were making. I just knew that it was "white," but not for long. My uncle Rowan got up into one of our fruit trees and in no time, we were enjoying a bowl of the most scrumptious hand-picked, hand churned peach ice cream. It was the beginning of a love affair.

From California to New Hampshire, from Boston to Lauderdale by-the-sea, and from Seattle to Monterey, California, the question is, what is *your* fave?

Cast my vote for the Revival Ice Cream company, a small, downtown shop, in Monterey, CA, creating from scratch, using sustainable locally sourced ingredients. My bestie: "Queen Bee," made from local beekeeper honey, with a hint of toffee and almonds, all harvested from the central coast.

Problem solved! All but one item... With Tigger in the store, no flavor is sustainable for long.

One Special Evening

I love what I do. I realize it often but there are moments when it fills me with joy and gratitude. My first fifty-years as an inspirational speaker have taught me so much. My celebration of this great adventure is not in what I can teach but in what I can learn. That evening was proof positive of the fact.

From the stage, I looked out at the audience with whom I had just shared the last two hours. They were standing up clapping and cheering, as I folded up my papers on the lectern. Many years ago, in the first days of my speaking career, I was foolish enough to think that the audience was clapping and cheering for me. The day I realized that our guests were celebrating themselves, was the best day of my professional career.

Supper time in a hotel, is not always a special occasion. Preparing a thousand-plus meals and setting them at table, is not an easy task but that evening, following a great connection with our seminar attendees, the meal was fantastic. A fine wine-bottle on the table, a fresh crisp salad, with a chilled fork and new wondrous friends to share. Filet Mignon broiled to perfection and served with real-mashed potatoes and green beans al dente, made this a fine repast. A wondrous ice cream confection from the chef's hands, a cup of delicious coffee and our day was perfect and almost complete.

Over the din of after dinner conversation and the clink and clank of table clearing, a familiar sound found my ears and my heart. I loved the film Charade and so the soundtrack had become an old familiar friend. The song that found me in the ballroom, was "Latin Snowfall," by Henry Mancini. I immediately rose from my seat, stepped toward the dance floor, and began to look for her. There, in her elegant red dress she stood. I realized how happy I was that I had learned the bolero... Won't you save me a dance?

Tigger

The Trestle (Part One)

Over the San Gabriel mountains, along the Angeles Crest Highway, we drove out of the Pasadena smog and up into the clear blue sky of a California Friday afternoon. We were going camping, and it was my first road trip behind the wheel of my dad's old '49 Pontiac. With a couple of my best friends and my prized learner's permit folded neatly in my wallet, I was the newly crowned king of the road. We were heading back to a place that my folks had shared with me as a lad. I was traveling on pure memory and the mind movies that had served me so well on foot, getting in and out of the California wilderness.

I was searching for a place where my family and I had camped, when I was a small boy. The site I remembered, was along a remote train track, up a sloping road to the foot of the Tehachapi mountains. As I recalled it, we could stand and look out for miles in all directions. My mom had taught me that our target practice should never endanger any other "Human" desert rats in the area. We needed to be truly alone; a spot where we could camp, hike, and discharge the firearms in my neato burrito collection.

I found it! Out of the thousands of square miles of the Mojave Desert, this one wonderful spot from my memory, came to life as we drove across the sage and greasewood and up to the old wooden railroad trestle. Once the door swung open, that fragrance brought all of my memories to life, and I was home. I could sweep the horizon with my eyes and see to the south, all the way to the snow-capped mountain range we had just crossed. To the east I could see the expanse of the Mojave Desert, which would one day soon, become the landing site for Space Shuttles. To the west, behind our campsite, I saw the Tehachapi Mountains that would serve as the canvas behind which the sun would set each afternoon. To the north we could marvel at five hundred miles of wild desert land, undisturbed and unoccupied. We were indeed alone. Time to start our campfire...

Tigger

The Trestle (Part Two)

The moment the sun dipped behind the mountains to our west, the temperature dropped a full thirty-degrees, and the wind began to whisper-cold. The crackling pine-wood fire felt good against the gathering desert night and our thoughts turned to mulligan stew.

My old blue Chevy Truck, "Tonka," as I had named her, was parked to serve as a wind break against the downslope wind and our sleeping bags were lined up like pea pods with our heads closest to the truck and our feet pointing out into the wild and wonderful desert. Our hope was, of course, when the kids were small, that we did not pee in our pods. As the beautiful southwestern night turned blue-black above us, the warm sleeping bags began to look like heaven. It was wonderful to realize that, since my first childhood visit, the desert was remote and foreboding enough to have remained pristine, primitive, and uncivilized.

Our first night, under the stars, was as wonderful as if Mister Disney himself had produced it. While we were doing our best to find our way to sleep, tiny kangaroo rats performed a ballet around us, and a coyote howled out a greeting to the slowly rising golden moon. I can't speak for my companions, but I found my way quickly to my repose and the promise of the day to come. It has always amazed me that awakening beneath the night sky in the heart of mother nature, reveals that the whole firmament moves in rotation, as if to confirm our place of wonder in the universe.

As I think back on it now, it's still a surprise to me, that over the years many of my friends chose not to join me in the magic and majesty of the wilderness whether desert, mountain, or beach. On this, my first grownup visit, I dreamed about having a family with whom I might share the wonder and magic of such a place as the trestle, in the great Mojave Desert.

The best is yet to come...
Tigger

The Trestle (Part Three)

T he Tehachapi Mountains are the demarcation point between the San Juaquin Valley and the Mojave Desert. They are also the backdrop for our annual Easter Campsite in the Mojave Desert. From my introduction as a small child, throughout all of the years since, we have made this spot our own. Adventures enough to fill a thousand pages, for certain.

Let's begin with crystal clear desert nights, decorated with so many shooting stars, there would be no way to count them all. Lined up in our cozy sleeping bags, we more-than-once fell asleep beneath the twinkling stars and awakened under a blanket of pure white snow. Our breakfast campfire was not only warm and fragrant but delivered hot coffee, bacon and eggs and a hearty serving of Sara Lee's pecan coffee cake.

Well-fed and camp properly policed, we would strike out, summer or winter, to wander for miles beneath the *"Lawrence of Arabia"* sun. We found so many artifacts which we brought back to camp for lunchtime show and tell. List: a complete covered wagon wheel, spokes, and all, which took us two days and four trips to drag back to camp, railroad spikes, miner's food store packages, bullet riddled pieces of tin and anything and everything else one can imagine, that might have found use on the wild and wonderful desert. On one particularly hot day, our first-born daughter came running up to me, breathlessly proclaiming, "Snake!" How right she was. Running across the burning sand, she had come upon and *jumped over* a huge rattle snake. We spent our sweltering afternoons beneath the old trestle, telling stories and exaggerating everything of course, all but the snake. That reptile needed no embellishment.

By evening we would get the campfire started and pull out our fireworks. The old trestle around which we camped, proved a perfect spot for launching firecracker rockets, up one side and down the other. Perfect for a game of, guess where it's coming down and try to catch it.

Tigger

The Trestle (Part Four)

Seventy-five years is a long time to expect a place to remain unchanged. I recall the times when the train would climb creaking along the rails next to our campsite and the brakeman would throw little bottles of "Railroad Water," off the caboose to us. We didn't need the water but the contact with a real railroad-man was as exciting as anything else we encountered in our desert hideaway. Imagine our surprise then, on one afternoon when he swung down off the train and came over to tell us that we could no longer camp there. It took me a while to catch my breath. I paused and took a long look at the young train man and guessed that on my first campout on this wild spot, this brakeman had not yet been born. Things were indeed changing.

Where once there was only sagebrush, greasewood, mesquite, creosote, jack rabbits, quail, doves, wood rats, crows, and pinyon pine, now just across the tracks, was a crew erecting power lines and the first of many wind turbines.

On one rainy Easter afternoon, in the last of our visits, we packed our gear and turned for home. All grown up now, we all lived in different directions. Thank heavens we were huggers and we held on tight. On our arrival home, a Highway Patrol officer was waiting on our Santa Barbara porch to inform us that our second born daughter had been killed in a hydroplane accident on the highway home.

Somewhere out there underneath the tower of a huge turbine generator, is our gigantic cast iron fry pan, a gift from our son Dave. Believing that we would always be coming back and to save the weight and space, we buried that rascal beneath the desert sand. One day soon I am going back, metal detector in hand, to retrieve our treasure and all of the memories that we had cooked up in it. I hope that you will come with me.

The long, lonely wail of a coyote, was our final goodbye to the trestle.

Tigger

Spellbound

Have you ever been transfixed? Have you ever felt charmed, enchanted, or entranced? When was it? Where were you? Were you alone, with a handful of friends or perhaps, part of a huge crowd? My answer would be yes to all of the above.

The opportunity to share a presentation with a large group of people, whether onstage or in the audience, is one of the most enchanting things one can ever experience. It has been my great honor to be invited to speak to audiences both large and small. That is how it was backstage in the Hilton Hotel, in Las Vegas Nevada. On the other side of the curtains two-thousand-plus attendees were enjoying their breakfast and awaiting the presentations that were to come. I was the second of those.

The master of ceremonies mounted the dais, tapped on the microphone, and called the room to order. This morning every word seemed to have special meaning for me, as I knew what was about to happen. The opening speaker was introduced to a rousing standing ovation and the flight began. His rich voice took us on a magic carpet ride, from incredible highs to devastating lows. He took us with him through the truth of sadness and the absolute joy of honest humor. He allowed us a deep look into his incredibly successful career and through it all, he shared a very powerful kind of inspiration.

I didn't realize it at first but as I listened, I became truly spellbound. As one who deeply loves my Country, I found myself falling in love again and seeing her with fresh eyes. I felt a clear and urgent call to serve once again. All of this in a matter of moments and then it was over. The audience, fresh from their own spellbound experience, was standing once again to honor our speaker. He came through the curtains and without a moment's hesitation, stuck out his hand to greet a complete stranger... Me!

It was the first and last time that I met General Colin Powell. I am still spellbound.

Tigger

Bill

It was a warm, early southwestern summer evening. The sun had just headed down behind the western wall of our canyon and I was typing away in my office when I heard a knock on our front door. I pulled open the portal, and there was our new neighbor, Bill. His large frame filled the doorway, and, in each hand, he carried a cocktail glass bearing two fingers of amber liquid.

Bill was a self-proclaimed recluse, so you can imagine my surprise at his visit. He was a friendly chap and a face-to-face encounter up on the mountain or out in the neighborhood, had always brought about a jovial exchange. Bill was a retired law enforcement guy and although he rarely spoke about his past employment, his discipline and character were obvious. He had stopped by to share a glass of his favorite, Pappy Van Winkle, fine bourbon. We went straight into my office, sat down, and began to sip and share a heart-to-heart conversation about life and its vicissitudes.

Perhaps like you, I take great stock in the way folks treat their critters. Along his way, Bill had picked up a tiny chihuahua which he named Mia. As dearly as I love animals, I've never had much truck with that breed, as they have a propensity to yip and yap and seem to take great joy in biting me. Somehow our neighbor had trained his little K9 to be a most wonderful creature. When we came upon each other out on the trail, Bill would turn Mia loose and she would come-a-running for some Doug loving, no matter how great the distance. I love that little pooch and it said something very special about my friend and his loving heart.

Bill took sick about two months ago and we were concerned about our friend. We didn't see him out and about at his beloved barbecue. His sister stopped by one day to share with us that Bill had Covid. One day, shortly thereafter, she asked us to reach out to 911... For Bill.

Then came the report that we had lost a very good man and dear friend.

Tigger
(R.I.P. Bill, Mia is in very good hands!)

The Call of Autumn

On Porters Lake, in Halifax, Nova Scotia, the afternoon shadows grow longer with each passing day. As if to say so long to a wonderful summer, a thin mist rises from the surface of the lake and climbs into the rising moon of a harvest evening. The lobster and ice-cold India pale ale, are a feast for friend and family alike.

To the south, in New Hampshire, Lake Winnipesaukee is slipping on her golden gown, as we dive down to release the anchor and tow away the swim platform. The joy of summer laughter and the fragrance of coconut tanning oil, seem to be exchanging places with the long sunset. Summer is turning the corner into autumn. What fun we have shared here.

Still farther south into the sunshine state, the attire chosen for our Mai-Tai's and grilled seabass on the deck of Aruba, has shifted away from sleeveless to sleeves. After a shared key lime pie and espresso, the call of the surf just beyond the sand, is not quite enough to draw us back for one last sunset ride. Things are changing and we will be putting the top up for the ride home across Las Olas Boulevard.

A World away and across our continent, the whisper of the Santa Ana wind through the Ponderosa Pines, with their long, graceful needles and jigsaw puzzle bark, seems to be fading. On the deck we inhale a hint of applewood smoke. Back inside the rustic a-frame, the old couple hardly notice the afternoon chill, as they pour a crisp Golden California Chardonnay into their waiting glasses. Thank you for the invitation.

In Kent Washington, as the young football player sweeps the leaves and dust from his family's porch, he imagines how one day very soon, the hay bales will be here as seats for the scarecrows. The pumpkins and jack-o-lanterns will be placed just here and the witch, who mysteriously appears every year about this time will be flying in such a way as to terrify trick-or-treaters who may choose to approach the festive and frightening entryway.

Across the North American continent, the imperious call of Autumn is clear and enticing...

Tigger awaits!

Without a Song!

The torch had come a long way... Beginning in New York City, the flame of the Olympiad was hand carried every step of the way, across more than nine-thousand miles and thirty-three states. The last of the courageous bearers was Gina Hemphill, a granddaughter of Jesse Owens, who carried the torch into the coliseum, completed a lap around the track, then handed it off to Rafer Johnson. Rafer was the winner of the 1960 decathlon Olympics. As the flame climbed the end of the great coliseum and the five rings ignited, the *"Olympic Fanfare and Theme"* filled the arena. It also filled the spirits of not only our nation but the world as well.

The now famous composer, John Williams, knew very well what he was striving for in his composition but I'm sure even he, could not imagine the power and impact of his music. Thirty-eight years later the world still finds the hair on their collective arms rising to salute that feeling. You can Google the music one day when you need a smidge of inspiration and, whatever your age, you will be transported to one of the great events in American history!

Long before those fabled Olympics, we were leaning against the wall of the Eliot Junior High gym, shuffling our feet, and trying hard not to make eye contact with the bonnie lasses across the floor. It was our spring *dance,* but I have always wondered why they didn't call it a *stand*. We seventh graders were quite sure that any attempt to invite a girl to dance would open the doorway to excruciating embarrassment. What if she says no??? What if she says yes??? Then it happened, the band that we had hired to provide our music, began to play and we were trapped. Our song was, *"Since I don't Have You,"* by the Skyliners. It was irresistible. What was the first song that ever dragged you away from your stand and into the arms of your first love?

Where would the Olympics be, without a song? For that matter where would M.A.S.H., Cheer's, Happy Days, or Mister Kotter be, without a song?

Tigger

Word Painter

As you can tell by reading these *"Desert Wind Chronicles,"* I have truly enjoyed every moment of my life here in this mysterious and beautiful southwestern desert. Sky above and earth below, as the Hopi express it. In the thousands of miles that I have wandered, I have celebrated the handiwork of the Great Spirit. A million canvases and colors. Simply entranced, I have never taken the time to try to name these wonders.

When Donovan composed the song, "Wear Your Love Like Heaven," I'm sure it never crossed his mind that he was unleashing a curiosity in me that would last a lifetime. Using an artist's exotic language, the singer-composer began to describe the colors that he was seeing around him. I was awakening to a whole new expression of the artiste's palette.

As a child, coloring with my Crayons, I came to know and recognize red, yellow, and blue. I was even aware of grey, pink and green but Prussian blue, rose carmethene and alizarin crimson were all new and exciting to me.

As inspiration always does for me, my friend Donovan Leitch had set me on a mind journey. Onyx, cerulean, teal, malachite, fandango wisteria and vermillion were one-and-all a wondrous new language for me.

The additive theory of color is based on human trichromatic vision, in which each primary color red, blue and yellow match up with the corresponding receptor cell in the human eye. We know now that we are perceiving colors as the combination of certain wavelengths of light.

I was fortunate enough to be chosen to record and sing a Donovan composition that was the theme song in the film *"If It's Tuesday This Must Be Belgium..."* I loved the opportunity and truly enjoyed hearing Donovan sing his beautiful "Lord of the Reedy River," in that movie. One day I will write a Desert Wind about George Harrison, Donovan Leitch, and The Maharishi. But that, as Rudyard Kipling wrote, is another story.

Tigger

The Battle at Glenwood

We were just finishing our limo ride when we pulled into the parking lot below Sandia Peak. The two old cowboys, sittin' in the back like we knew what we were doing, were witness to the show from the beginning.

Our driver, a fine fellow who had made our day a marvelous one, was buttoned up in his compartment, with the window between us rolled up tight. From our seats in the back of our beautiful buggy we heard a voice from outside the limo say, "You better move that thing out of here!" Our driver responded very courteously, "We're doing just fine. Move along Sir..." There wasn't even a hint of challenge in our driver's voice, but the chap pressed on. "I said you better get that thing out of here right now!" All of this before our driver even put down his window. Once again, in a very gentle voice, our man responded, "We're not hurting anything, I suggest that you move along!" The antagonist kept it up, "You're breaking the law! Now get that fancy machine out of here!"

Up until now, our driver was unruffled an absolute gentleman. The antagonist with a raised and aggressive voice, began to shriek at our driver using the most vulgar language. Our fellow asked, "are you an officer?" "No, but I can call one!" Our driver responded, that perhaps it would be the best thing. When the playground bully yelled at the top of his lungs, "You better get that piece of crap and whatever idiots you are dragging around in it, out of here before there is trouble!"

This insulting language toward his passengers, was the straw that broke the camel's back. Our driver jumped out of his door and moved quickly, face to face and chest to chest with our antagonist.

With this confrontation, loud-mouth, in a state of shock, quickly backed off, changed his tone and his tune. It would seem that he saved himself from real danger and a visit with the local gendarmes. Being as how we two cowboys were passengers and audience to the confrontation, let us finish this adventure with an old country expression.

"Don't interfere with somethin' that ain't botherin' you none!"

Friends

"**H**ow come you are so dang cheerful?" It was a simple question. The game was over, my team had lost, and we were heading into the kitchen for a sandwich and a modest libation. I have, for most of my adult days, tried to figure ways to live in some form of celebration, whatever the winds of life might deliver and so it was that I was happy and content to watch today's football game, win or lose. I am a hopeless positive thinker or as my long-time pal Hank calls it, a positive stinker.

Back on the couch, my guest sipped at the head of his Tsing Tao beer, took a deep breath, and began the interrogation in earnest. "I mean, you love football more than anyone I know. You have your favorite team or teams and yet when they lose, you are as cheerful as if they had blown out their opponent... What gives?" I begged for a few moments to think it out, dug deeply into my bean dip, munched on a handful of corn chips, and responded: "Having travelled around America for so many years, I have frequented every football city there is. I have visited nearly every stadium, watched, and celebrated some of the greatest players of all time and cheered myself hoarse. In each of these cities I have friends whose love for their team is over the top. I'm talking scream and holler, get a little tipsy and sometimes throw a little money down on their boys. I could tell by his face that he still didn't seem to connect with my explanation, so I tried one more time: "Here's the deal... Because I have dear friends in every football city in the country, I have reason to celebrate when their teams win even if, from time to time, they happen to be putting a whuppin on my team...

So that, my faithful readers is the reason that I am so dang cheerful. Under *any* circumstances I am a winner and that makes me happy! Hooray!

Tigger

Grateful

It was well into the sunrise when I met these two strangers. They, coming up Doug's Mountain and I, on my way down. Nicely dressed as hiking attire goes and bringing their large golden pooch along with them, we stopped to share a howdy. "First time up?" I asked. "Yep," was their brief but friendly retort. They had come from their home in Anthem to share our mountain trail and they were mighty impressed. As we stood, six feet apart, looking out over the beautiful Las Vegas Valley, I spotted another new face about twenty feet to our left. It was a young cooper's hawk, working feverishly to extract his prey from a rather large cholla cactus. (Can you say choy-yuh?)

This beauty was an easy spot in the bright morning light, with his steely blue-gray upper body and shoulders, red eyes, and the familiar warm reddish bars across his proud chest. When I pointed him out to my new friends, we all paused to watch his activities. I mentioned that if we watched long enough, he would, at some point with his powerful short wings, suddenly flap three or four times and begin a long fast glide down the desert mountainside. "And why would he do that?" the lady asked curiously. I explained that, though I was no expert, his hunting style was to glide at very high speed over the ground and then rapidly crest a bush, or an outcropping of rock, to drop down on the other side and pounce upon an unsuspecting bird or critter. Voila, lunch!

I was "grateful" to meet these new friends and wondered, looking back, if they had ever tasted the wine by that name? "Grateful!" It comes from "Cooper's Hawk," a Canadian winery and fine restaurant. It might just be a fine thanksgiving American or Canadian tasting opportunity.

I see our cooper's hawk often now and truly enjoy watching him on the hunt or dining on his capture. "à Votre santé!"

Tigger

Accents

It was a bright, cool morning on the trail and to a desert rat like me, thirty-seven degrees seemed mighty brisk. The clear November sun was a blessing and like the song says, it was shining so my nose wouldn't freeze. Although one of the great joys of my mountain is the absence of foot-traffic, voices, and human noise, it is always a pleasure to share my solitude during a chance encounter.

His was not a face that I recognized. "Good morning Sir!" I offered and his response was immediate, "Good day to you..." A voice raised in another land was a pleasant addition to our trail. I love accents. They are a way to help identify the stranger before us. Given the opportunity, I copy my dad's expression of greeting, "Where do you hail from stranger?" he would ask. My new friend's response was, "England actually, some time ago." His voice was soft, as is often the case with those from the U.K. His pronunciation was smooth and gracious. My question, "whereabouts in England?" "London," he replied. He sounded like a Londoner and I should know, my dad was a scouse, or as he put it, a "Liverpudlian" from the town where the Beatles grew up.

In a nation that is built upon the arrival of immigrants I always find it hard to countenance the level of prejudice that exists here. Whenever the situation arises, particularly with Latinos and middle easterners, I look for *genuine* reasons to share a sense of welcome and recognition. Whether in a limo or a store, I enjoy the opportunity to say, "That's a fine accent..." And I like to add, "Your English is beautiful as well!" I am aware of the effort and commitment it takes to conquer not only the words of a foreign language but the dialect, pronunciation and inflection that makes us understandable one to another. Welcome friend...

Tigger

Contact

"*H*ello, my dear friend and thank you... Like an astronomer awaiting a response to a message sent out in a cosmic bottle, my hope was that some life form out in the galaxy, would receive my message, and reach out in return. Although any news is important and constructive criticism is the life blood of a writer, my fondest wish is that the response may be a positive one. You have done all of this for me. I am touched, encouraged, and inspired! Thank you from the bottom of my heart." These are my exact words sent in response to the following note from my dear friend and reader Tom, from Lynchburg, VA. "Doug: Loved the book and enjoyed the read. As I was reading, I thought you gave a new meaning to living life. Most people just say it in passing but you LIVE IT for real!!! It is an honor to call you friend." Me too, you, Tom!

Writing is a lonely business. We who spend a year or more at the desk, crafting our words into stories, are owed no response and that is how it should be. I write the book, you buy the book, and that is that. So, I had no idea how much I wished for that contact, until Tom's message arrived and as I read his words the hair on my arms stood on end.

We earthlings are uniquely different from one another and in my life, I have tried very hard to be a real thank you kind of guy. It is surely not something I expect of others and so I was surprised by my response to those of you who made it a point to reach out to make contact. I loved it. In the days of covid and politics we are starved for uplifting conversation, handshakes, hugs, and fresh air.

My new book, "Sunlight and Shadows," (A Manual for living Life!) is available from Amazon.com, and I would be honored if you would order my book!

I love you,
Tigger

Lost

Alone in the mist and midst of the Christmas dawn he sat, back straight, eyes shining, barely old enough to walk. It was only to his parents that he was lost. Vibrantly alive and curious he found himself in a perfectly directed adventure.

The first breeze of morning came whispering up the hillside and into the meadow. The tallest shafts of grass bowed gracefully in thanks for the invitation to dance. The boy's tiny nostrils gave thanks too, for the joyous fragrance born on the wind. His young mind new not the names from the books or the words from the school, to describe the fragrance. Juniper, bay laurel, sweet pine, lichen, and heather were incense enough to fill a whole mountaintop. As new to the world as he was, he could sense that glory was here.

The earth, round his little blond head was motion and color and these new eyes were entranced.

From above, the clear sweet call of a tiny feathered soloist, passing through the endless blue frame, brought little hands into the air reaching so gently. Not begging come back for the capture but asking only to be taken along on the winged journey or at least left with the secret of flight.

In the gathering light of dawn, a thistle bloom decorated with moisture, made rainbows of dew drops and beckoned young fingers to touch. From the leaf to the lips, the child brought one diamond drop of the precious life-giving liquid, and the spell was complete.

Here, in this enchanted place, with the warmth of the sun on his little back, in the arms of the Great Father of the Forest, the boy nodded and fell asleep.

Silently the great, warm golden ball of energy rose into the morning sky. "Where are you son?" came his father's voice. Then, in an instant, the shadows, the secrets, and the tiny woodland creatures who had shared his worship, disappeared into the moment and the moment was gone forever.

Bless you,
Tigger

Magic

J ust outside my office window is a mountain. This is not just any mountain but a magnificent edifice worthy of its birthright. It is a fifteen-million-year-old volcano. Most days of the week, whatever season, and weather you will find me climbing to the top. This is not only *my mountain,* but it is my friend, guide, companion, and my theater. The act of learning and experiencing is where we discover the deeper magic from the dawn of time.

Many times, in these chronicles of ours, I have mentioned "old man coyote." He was here when this mountain first erupted, and he will be here when it comes to life again. What do we know about these intriguing and entertaining "Song Dogs?" "Nahuatl," as the Aztecs so named the breed thousands of years ago, were the first to identify these members of the canine family. Coyotes are associated with the character "Coyote," which holds an important place in the mythology and religion of multiple indigenous groups in North America. He is known for his attempts to manipulate other animals and beings. To the Navajo, Coyote is an important figure in the creation of the world. He represents both good and evil. They use sounds to communicate, including yips, barks, and howls, as well as scent and visual signs.

So it was, on a late autumn afternoon, very near the top of my mountain, that I caught a glimpse of old man coyote's magic. We often walk together, aware of one another but not interfering in each other's journey. As we reached the late afternoon shadow, my companion simply disappeared into the mountain. It was as if David Copperfield had watched us and decided to confirm the art of the trickster.

I find great joy in believing in mysterious and wonderful things. This was simple proof of something I had heard about and studied but never seen. I wondered, where did he go? Just inside the mountain or into a time warp? I am not one who needs to figure out and understand everything I see. I simply enjoy reveling in the questions left behind. Powerful Medicine.

Tigger

Bemelmans Bar

Tommy Smothers had sent me off to New York City to assist Joan Cooney and the "Children's Television Workshop," in their negotiations with a group of record companies. As vice president of the Smothers' record company, my assignments varied but this was one that I truly relished. Where else could an executive cowboy go, to end up with the friendship of none other than Jim Henson and Super Grover.

The Brothers were kind enough to put me up in their apartment in one of New York's old prestigious hotels and it was a week of wonders. Heading back "home" from my day's labors, I discovered that in the lobby of the luxurious Carlyle, was a famous watering hole, piano bar, and meeting place. In honor of the age of my accommodations, I ordered a Wild Turkey Old Fashioned. Delicious!

In these days, laced with hatred, prejudice and anger, I am always searching for times and places that provide the opportunity for human connection. New York watering holes do just that. A warm atmosphere, fireplace, piano-bar, and fine cocktails to loosen the spirit and you have it! That brings me to Bemelmans. With masterpiece murals by Ludwig Bemelmans, the creator of the classic Madeline children's books, Bemelmans bar draws socialites, politicians, movie stars and moguls. The extensive drink menu and live entertainment keep the place packed.

We live now in the Tik Tok generation. However, you picture the members of this group, I can tell you that they have a very sophisticated side. Along with creating the future, they are truly fascinated with the past. These twenty-somethings come into Bemelmans, to rub shoulders with eighty-year-old patrons who have been sipping martinis and singing American-standards there, since the nineteen-fifties. This is my kind of place!

"Play me a song, mister piano man..." Make mine an old, fashioned!

Tigger

Eagles (Part One)

Her question was a simple one: "If I bring my wheelchair, will I be a bother?" My response was just as simple: "It will be an honor!" We were heading into the Wasatch Mountains for the Gathering of Eagles retreat. Old friends and new friends from across the North American continent had signed on to join us and social media was alive with the smoke signals of our excitement.

When Bob and I made the commitment, we had only the slightest inkling of what was to come. We could not have imagined the wonders that were to be the rewards for our idea and efforts. We were giving birth to a miracle.

Once on the mountain, Snowbird Lodge, we met in the meadow around the huge welcome fire, to connect and find our way out of the world we had left behind. We began to merge into the spirit world of the Eagles. One of our guests arrived on wheels and true to our conversation, there was never a moment that anything slowed down or changed course because of Dottie.

There were many adventures and stories to be told about the gathering but this one had to wait until just now and you shall see why. The "Vision Walk," was a special exercise that called upon participants to completely change their perceptions and the use of their senses. We started at the bottom of the ski run and walked across the river bridge together. Once above the rushing water, we were instructed to stand just apart, reach into our minds and one by one lift out the thoughts found there. We then tossed them gently into the creek. Our guests, some seventy strong, each took their time to do as they were instructed. Their success could be measured by the time they each spent on the bridge above the creek.

We were beginning a journey that would change us all forever... Some far more than others. To be continued...

Tigger

Eagles (Part Two)

We left the bridge with clear instructions, that until we crossed the bridge on our return, we were not to speak. No matter what we saw or heard, those visions and sounds were for us and us alone. Our first test came no more than fifty yards into the forest, when a beautiful mule deer stepped out of the trees and into a clearing. The electricity ran through our group. Look! See! Do you see what I see? If I don't tell you what I am seeing, you will miss it! More than one of our fledglings had to be motioned to be still and enjoy.

The trail led from the creek bridge, up through a beautiful white fir forest. Our way was studded with rocky mountain maple, boxelder, and mountain mahogany. As if our senses were not already over stimulated, the fragrance of staghorn lichen was like wild incense for our noses. With new eyes, we watched rabbits, coyotes, porcupines, raccoons, badgers, and pika. All the while we were no doubt being watched by elk, mountain lions and bobcats and eagles.

The trees above us were filled with raptors and birds. In our silence their songs became clear, distinct, and joyful. Even the comings and goings of their wings, gave forth a sweet symphony to our awakened ears. All the while our silent sisters and brothers sipped their water and drank in, those things their human noises had for years unknowingly shut out. Back on the bridge we welcomed the hot perspired, thirsty overwhelmed newborn Eagles. It was a sweet goodbye for all of us, enlightened one by the other.

Three weeks later we received a wonderful handwritten note from our newest Eagle. She said: "I have never shared what I am about to share with you. On our Eagle journey, I found the kind of friends and family it takes to bare one's soul and move beyond the abuses of our lives. Those hurts are now in the river beneath the bridge on the Vision Walk. They will never hurt or haunt me again. Bless you. Dottie" (07/23/1932-01/12/2021)

Bats

If I were to ask you to name the only flying mammal, how would you respond? A few more clues: It is nicknamed sky-puppy, travels by night, is very mysterious, has great ecological value, eats insects by the bushel and sleeps upside down. I knew you would get it. If you answered *Die Fledermaus* you are correct. The operetta name translates into "The Flitter Mouse!" or the bat.

What brought about this sudden interest in bats? Our dear friends and neighbors brought me a very special birthday gift. It was a bat. A real Louisville Slugger and I've always wanted one.

Each evening, in the setting sun, our monastery sky begins to fill with these wonderful little creatures. We sit in wonder as they dart about in the dusk, radar fixing on an insect and then diving in for the capture. One less mosquito and here in Nevada that means we have only one of these pests left.

Visiting our friends, the Halls, in Austin Texas, we finished our fine Mexican meal and margarita... How does one say yummy en Espanol? These dear friends are youthful, vigorous, and adventuresome so I got the feeling that something was a foot when, after supper, we were hustled into their buggy and driven off as if we were in a presidential motorcade. We were on our way to view the world-famous Austin's "Birds of the Night." One and a half million Mexican Free Tail bats. These good guys of the night sky eat about twenty-thirty thousand pounds of insects a night... Thank you!

Recently, a dear friend saw me holding my new slugger lovingly and commented: "I thought that you were a prayin' man!" My response, "I am indeed... The bat is just here to make sure I get what I'm praying for!

Tigger

Football

It was a cool autumn afternoon, and we were sharing a fireside recliner, football kind of afternoon when my dear friend turned to me and queried: "How come you are so dang cheerful?" It was a simple question, and I realized why he asked. The game was over, my team had lost, and we were heading into the kitchen for a sandwich and a modest libation. As an inspirational person I have spent most of my adult days trying to figure ways to live in some form of celebration whatever the winds of life might deliver. And so it was that I was happy and content to watch today's football game, win or lose.

Back on the couch my guest sipped at the head of his Tsing Tao beer, took a deep breath, and began the interrogation in earnest. "I mean, you love football more than anyone I know. You have your favorite team or teams and yet when they lose you are as cheerful as if they had blown out their opponent... What gives?" Having never thought of this before, I begged for a moment to think it out, munched on a handful of corn chips, scooped deeply into the guacamole, and responded.

Having travelled around America for so many years I have frequented every football city there is. I have visited many stadiums watched and celebrated some of the greatest players of all time and cheered myself hoarse. In each of these cities I have friends whose love for their team is over the top. I'm talking scream and holler, get a little tipsy and sometimes throw a little money down on their "boys."

He didn't seem to connect with my revelation, so I went on. "Here's the deal... Because I have dear friends in every football city in the country, I have reason to celebrate with them and for them whenever their team wins. The light of understanding began to dawn in his eyes.

What he didn't know was that it was the birth of a new understanding for me too. By celebrating with and for others, my spirit was not diminished in sharing the glory with others.

The Trickster

Some years ago, camped on the top of our Spiritsong Ranch, in the Rocky Mountains, we were heading off to dreamland in the back of Tonka our blue chevy truck. Looking up, our view of the clear, moonless starlit summer sky, was framed by a stand of tall, ancient, aspen trees. Cozy in our sleeping bags, around two am, Mike, our Aussie shepherd, camped at our feet, let out a deep soft growl. Our faithful dog was a great early warning system for such critters as bears and coyotes. No sooner had our pooch sat up, when the sweet voice of "Canis Latrans" let out his familiar howl. With that, our protector and guardian leapt out of the truck bed and hit the ground running. Barking his head off, he raced into the woods toward the sound. Coyotes rarely harm humans but they do find dogs and cats to be a tasty treat. Here's how they pull it off.

The lead coyote discovers, by smell alone, that a pet creature is near at hand and stations him or herself about fifty yards away from the campsite and the ashes of the evening's campfire. They then howl a plaintive, un-threatening call. The faithful dog jumps up to protect master and family and heads off into the woods. This is where it gets interesting.

Coyote number two is just a bit deeper in the woods and takes over the song. These tricksters keep up this charade, one after the other, until your doggie is too deep in the forest to be rescued and then the pack surrounds him and makes short work of your companion.

One of the joys of owning an Australian Shepherd, besides their beautiful coat and fiercely loyal disposition, is their marvelous obedience. Once loved and trained, this marvelous working creature will do anything to please his master. On this exciting rocky mountain night, I let Mike have his head for about fifty-yards and I simply said, "Mike Come," and out of the forest, a very proud and wiggly guardian returned for his reward. Mike lived to protect us many times thereafter.

Tigger

Discoveries

I n a recent Desert Wind, I wrote about the common, fascinating patterns that appear in nature. Not only did my readers tell me that they enjoyed this story but they have added to my knowledge and let me know they want more. Here we go.

From Newport, Rhode Island, to the lush gardens of La Jolla, California, I have crawled, creeped, climbed and stared into the faces of flowers. Sunshine or thunder, as a photographer I travel this wonderful water planet, trying my best to capture the colors and character of these blooms, blossoms, and their curious little visitors.

In every case, from the first click, to today's snaps, I have always felt I was letting my heart guide my eye and my spirit decide when to click the shutter. Recently I began to realize, it is the flowers that have been allowing me to come along on these adventures. They, it seems, are the artists and I am the student.

In corresponding with my dear friend Dr. DiSalvo, the great chemist, I found that he and I share a common bond, in that our long suit is not mathematics. I also found that the art and science of our labors has led us to the fountain of numbers. From his creations of exquisite beauty products, to my photos of nature, the numbers are there. When the Italian mathematician,

Fibonacci, of Pisa, first laid out the Fibonacci sequence, or golden ratio, he was guiding us in locating the most aesthetically pleasing arrangement for our dance, composition, painting, hairstyle, or photograph. His Golden Ratio is found everywhere in nature and creation.

If we study the design of a nautilus shell, pinecone, artichoke, sunflower, dandelion or any one of the flower photos in my collection, we find that it is this magic design that captures and holds our sense of wonder. Recently I was surprised to discover that I have more than ten-thousand images of these wonders up there in that cloud. My joy has been in discovering that the flower is the master and I am the entranced apprentice.

Tigger

El Pipo

The class was in the beautiful Sheraton Universal hotel, in Universal City California. There were sixteen of us and I was lucky enough to be the teacher. Inside the royally draped meeting room, we sat at a closed conference table, seven at a side and one at each end. John Olsen was at the foot of the table and I stood at the head, with a lovely polished wooden lectern lighted for my notes.

This was not a program that I had sold to my guests, this was a training requested by the barbers who served as trainers for the men's division of this young, powerful beauty company. Something about my early presentations had caught their eye and they wanted to put some polish on their own performances. The names are mostly gone now but Paul DiSalvo, Bob Bartolac, John Olsen, Byron Niles, and Hector Barragan were in attendance. It had not crossed my young over-confident mind, but I was about to learn far more than I taught in my first NORTHSTAR communication training.

I had provided a handsome workbook for each of my guests and to encourage and facilitate note taking I had given each a felt tip pen. About twenty minutes into the class, I noticed that the tips of the pens made a swishing sound as they wrote and that one of my classmates was taking a long time to finish each entry in the journal. It was Hector Barragan, and it took me a bit to realize that this brilliant businessman, from El Paso, Texas was listening and taking in every thought and English word that I spoke, translating into his native Spanish and then writing it down for future use. I never forgot this lesson.

Hector is one of the most recognized business owners and leaders in El Paso. He is a master educator and, in days gone by, a matador. Hence his name in the title above: "El Pipo..." Hector is still a dear friend and much loved by his El Paso neighbors.

Tigger

Compose

One of my favorite CDs of all time was created and performed by Van Morrison. It was titled "Poetic Champions Compose," and for my money, the songs were some of his best. The music, like the lyrics, seemed to reach across the canyon of earthly love and connect with something so much greater on the other side. The songs touched me deeply and found their way into our seminar music. "Did Ye Get Healed, Spanish Steps and my favorite, Someone Like You." The CD was a gift from a now departed friend. I think all of us who ever wrote a song or dreamed of writing a song, have wished to be a Poetic Champion. So it was, on that Santa Barbara afternoon.

Two guitars, a fire in the firepit and a fine glass of wine. This memory often comes to mind as the year turns toward autumn. On our patio the view out to the blue pacific was clear and inspiring. Surrounded by the fragrance of pine smoke, George and I let the afternoon carry us into the moment.

As we sat and sipped, we chatted about the fact that the recorded music we were hearing on the radio, had taken a turn to the dark side from the sweetness and heart of our beloved sixties . Even the instrumentation had headed off into a raspy and minor mood. Not bad music, just on the negative side. "Let's create our own piece," I said. "Lay it on me" George responded.

My first two lyrics were, "Maybe Today," and we strummed and harmonized until the evening closed in around us. "Maybe Today will be my day, the day I've waited so long for." As if to share the reason and inspiration for our tune, I wrote, "Didn't I see the sun this morning, pouring down through the trees, spilling patterns on the street, to be dried off by the breeze!"

There were twelve-hundred wonderful people in the ballroom of the Sheraton Universal on that special evening, including the friend who had given me the CD. Mics in hand, we walked through the audience and climbed to the stage where our band was rocking out behind us. As we sang the title to close out our performance, we knew by the cheers and the standing ovation we had crafted a song worthy of a poetic champion!

Rags and Blossom (Doug and George)

Gone Away

It was a bumpy ride from Denver (DEN) to Wichita (ICT) on a United seven-thirty-seven. I love to fly and always try to find my way to a window seat. After all of these years and millions of miles in the air, I am still fascinated by the land that drifts by below me. On board, you will most often find me in seat 1A, left hand side of the aircraft, nose pressed up against the window.

I am returning to the place where my pal was born and raised; one of "them farm boys," as Jonathon Winters used to call him. In the time it takes to collect your bags, and head out onto state route four hundred, across the great plains of America, the time machine begins keeping time. I am fortunate to be one of those folks who loves wherever I am. I love the landscape, the people, the customs, the food and in the case of Kansas, the warm south wind, that on a warm summer afternoon can make your flight mighty bumpy.

Pretty Prairie is a tiny town all by its lonesome in the heart of the prairie. My friend and I had come a year earlier to film the world-famous rodeo in this town of five-hundred people. Having driven in on our last visit, we headed east from downtown Denver and almost immediately found ourselves in the land of Colby Kansas. The place where John Denver wrote and sang about his uncle Matthew. Within a half hour drive east bound, just as it was west bound from Wichita, we began to see old farmhouses and barns, empty, deserted, and derelict. Steve and I would stare in silence as we drove by these beautiful old buildings. We rode in deep meditation on what we were seeing.

Who were the people that journeyed to this place, where did they come from, what were their hopes and dreams and what gave them the courage and fortitude to build these places of refuge in the land of Oz?

Without having ever met them, I know these people. I know them because they are me and you. I know them because so many of the places that I have lived in and loved, have fallen to the grim reaper of progress. The Ranch, in Los Altos Hills, California, an original early adobe, 44 Yankee Point Road, below Clint Eastwoods place on Mal Paso, and our beautiful childhood home, Fox Ridges, in Altadena, California. These are places to which I can lead you but like the residents who once called these places home they are *gone away*. I miss the fragrance and glory of these them all.

Tigger

High Rise

"Whatcha lookin' at?" The voice was friendly and familiar. Early autumn mornings in MacDonald Ranch bring out the best in the people, the weather and nature. On this morning's walk, I had paused to examine a giant rosemary bush, when my neighbor stopped to inquire about my doings. During our discussion, I mentioned that by observing the size of this rosemary bush, along the side of the trail, I knew it must be nearly a quarter of a century young. At ten feet tall and forest green, it was a beauty.

The fall seems to suit our greenery, as this bush was radiant in color and rich in fragrance. I mentioned how, when grilling out, I would toss a sprig or two of this aromatic bush onto my barbecue to enrich the flavor of the meal and to completely eliminate any insects that might be flying around in wait for the meal service. That includes mosquitos! In my thirty-five plus years in Nevada, I have never received one mosquito bite.

I revealed to my visitor, that I looked at this ancient, verdant bush, much like a huge tenement building. During the fall bloom, her balconies of purple blossoms are a beautiful gathering place for our precious pollinators. The air is truly buzzing with sound and energy. They circle and land again and again to reload their furry legs with this life-giving magic.

Many times, I have had the pleasure of observing "Rosemary Manor," when butterflies came to visit. Beautiful white desert marble, gray hairstreak, mormon fritillary, and orange sulfur butterflies landed just inches from my curious face. Such beauty and grace.

My favorite, I explained to my guest, had just been days before, when I observed what appeared to be a little face peering out from an opening in the shrubbery. On closer inspection it revealed itself to be a side blotched lizard. No doubt the caretaker for the manor. On your next visit, remind me to give you a tour of "Rosemary Manor..."

Tigger

The Blue Bar

It had been a rare and snowy winter in the high Sierras. The melt of early summer had brought a beautiful and welcome torrent of runoff down the hillsides, to where we were wading into the King's River. Don't start with me! I have heard the lecture from park rangers and strangers alike, about the dangers of icy cold rushing water. I truly harken to the risks but there are some adventures in life that are worth the risk. Our two lovely ladies, perched on the boulder in the middle of the river just above us were the prize. If they were not enough, the bottle of Dry Sack that they had placed tantalizingly on the rock face between them, set the hook and Jim and I began the swim upstream to meet our beauties. Like spawning salmon, we made our way upstream to our rendezvous.

The high mountain afternoon summer sun was a warm and a welcome shivering change from the 46-degree water. I'm sure that the pair of redtail hawks circling above us and looking down between the mighty Whitebark, Foxtail pines and redwood giants, must have wondered at the strange pale creatures below.

Now add to this cool and remote location the following swimming holes: Maho Bay, Saint John Virgin Islands, The Little Susitna River, Alaska, The Firehole River in Yellowstone, Two Medicine Falls in Glacier National Park, Montana, C.B.'s beautiful "Carpe

Diem," in Lake Winnipesaukee, New Hampshire and the Rainbow River in Dunellen, Florida and you have a small sample of the wonderful places that have embraced me in their watery wonders.

All of these have become more than a swimming hole to me. They have become a place of refuge and refreshment. They are, at sunrise and sunset, a place of holy communion and baptism. Where it was permitted and encouraged, these were my bathing places. Thanks to my fine longtime friend, Dr. Ron, I have carried and put to good use a fragrant little item from my backpack simply titled "The Blue Bar!

A clean, refreshed Tigger

The Sycamores

Reaching up into the turquoise Sedona sky, these beauties seem to be stretching their limbs in preparation for a canyon ballet. To sit in meditation on the bench at their base, one would never realize that these wonders were here for a hundred years before this exquisite courtyard was constructed. Tlaquepaque is magic. Pronounced, "T-La-Keh-Pah-Keh," which means the "best of everything," this Mexican style village is a southwestern dream. From the beautifully crafted stone arch entry way and throughout, along the cobblestone paths, every view is a wonder. It is an artists' wonderland.

A favorite memory for me, is our first visit with our youngest son. He, having an exceptional artist's eye, was entranced by the carvings and paintings in every gallery and window. When we reached the point in our wanderings that we became a little twelve o'clock-ish, we decided on Mexican food; tableside guacamole accompanied by a fresh handmade margarita. To our surprise, our son, all of seven years old and a true lover of Mexican cuisine, begged to remain outside, to continue his artist's tour. Our luncheon at El Rincon was fantastic. We made sure to order something special to carry out for our young Diego Rivera and we found him right where we left him, sitting at the base of the ancient sycamore tree and staring up into her branches. We led him to an appropriate bench, handed over his chile rellenos and began to listen to him unwind his adventures for us. It was truly wonderful. He was so taken by the place, that he appeared to be hypnotized. He spoke in a mystical, far away voice, as if he had been teleported into another realm. His report was neither childish nor childlike but studied and clearly enunciated for us. He concluded his story by sharing he had picked out one piece of art that he wanted for his own. It was a beautiful oil painting priced modestly at $7000. We bought him an oil painting kit and agreed to cheer him on. He is still a great artist and we still love Sedona...

Tigger

Wright-Rite-Right

*"T*he longer I live, the more beautiful life becomes..." The renowned artist and architect, Frank Lloyd Wright, said it so very well... For one of the great adventures of my life, I was fortunate enough to live a taste of his extraordinary design skill.

It was during my joyful radio days at KRLA, in Pasadena, California when we set out to find a place to live. My imagination had always been captured by certain terms and this classified ad covered it all: "On a hill, overlooking the valley, above it all, unique construction, an artist's dream..." For some reason, the name of the architect was not mentioned.

So it was that we started up, out of the smoggy San Gabriel Valley and onto the Angeles Forest Highway. This was a piece of my childhood, as three generations of Cox's had spent many a Friday afternoon, driving up this road to Charlton Flats, where at fifty-four-hundred feet elevation, our family would unpack our old Studebaker, to set up camp and share the mountain air, the campfire, and the fellowship.

The realtor had agreed to meet us at the property and the further up we drove, the more my heart raced at what I saw. As I turned into the driveway, the canary pines that surrounded the home, were waving a welcome. At first, I just wanted to sit in my old caddy and take in the sights. I wanted a taste of what I would see on my arrival home from work. By the look of the entryway and the lines of the home front, I knew. This was a Frank Lloyd Wright home.

A Frank Lloyd Wright designed residence requires more than one Desert Wind to share. Suffice to say that roasting marshmallows with our kids on the built-in fireside bench, or sharing a song with our friends John Stewart and Buffy Ford, beside the pool overlooking all of Southern California, was a dream for Mrs. Cox's little boy, Tigger

Smile

As the calendar moves rapidly toward the holidays, our minds and our hearts turn toward happy times. I love this time of year because the moon seems to be smiling... I guess with so many challenges both health wise and politics *not so wise,* the $64,000 question is, why? In our wonderful neighborhood, I can think of a few very good reasons for a smile.

Our neighbor and friend, Bill, is one good sized rascal. With his history in law enforcement, he looks a lot like a lineman for his favorite team, The Buffalo Bills. Perhaps the moon is smiling because the Bills are playing very well this season... Yay!

Next, Bill's sis owns a huge Great Dane with the sweetest demeanor, so one might think that when Big Bill got a hankering to adopt, he would choose a Bull Mastiff, a Saint Bernard or some such, but no! I think the moon smiles when our neighbor's beast comes out of his house to take Bill for a walk and we realize that Bill owns a tiny little chihuahua named Mia. She is a treasure, no bigger than a minute and we love her.

One last reason for a lunar grin might just be that as Bill went out of his house a few weeks ago, he stopped to inform us that he was off to buy a new car. For all of the days since he joined our neighborhood, we have enjoyed seeing him depart and return from the market or Tucson in his big shiny truck. Imagine our surprise when he returned, "Meep-Meep," in a tiny Le Car, perhaps the smallest of all conveyances.

Smiles don't arrive on United Parcel! They are happening every moment around us and it is our responsibility to observe, enjoy and then share them.

Thanks for the friendship and the smiles!

Tigger

The Chase

It was a beautiful autumn morning. The sky above the vast Las Vegas Valley, was cobalt blue and I could see forever. Heading down from my morning climb, I was walking very carefully. Carrying my brand-new birthday camera, I made sure to place each step in such a way that I did not slip on the shale pathway. I had already made a pact with myself, that if I were to go down, I would take the fall and save my camera. At the bottom of the trail, I realized that I had only snapped six frames onto my empty memory card. Other than the beautiful horizon and the world-famous city below, I had not seen anything that inspired my shutter finger.

Turning up the road, toward our home, I spotted a movement on the desert floor. Whatever it was, matched the color of the landscape and as not to lose my lock on the target, I kept my eyes fixed as I moved closer. Ears! It was a cottontail hiding at the bottom of a cholla cactus. A perfect spot for a prey animal. Sheltered by a crown of the nastiest of thorns, this little furball was on the run from something that had a rabbit breakfast on his menu.

I didn't have to wait long to identify his assailant. Out of the blue, and like a streak of lightning, swooped a Coopers Hawk. Known for their flying skill and agility, her plumage was striking in the bright morning sun light. Impervious to the treacherous thorns, she landed on the top of the cactus. She had chosen a perch from which she left her breakfast no easy escape route. From my position, a brand-new camera glued to my eye, I could see clearly, both predator and prey.

Suddenly the young rabbit broke cover and raced down the hill and into the open. I watched as he zigged and zagged and his pursuer swooped ever closer. By now my readers have chosen sides and begun to root for one or the other. Just as the tawny breakfast snack was at deaths door, he dove into a burrow, leaving the mighty raptor in an empty desert. Back in my office I sat looking at a dozen of the worst photos of my career. I will learn!

Tigger

The Harvest

When we left our home on the Spiritsong, the temperature was a modest twenty-two degrees. The wind at nine thousand feet, was a hooter right out of the north pole and the snow was swirling and dancing around us. We were off on an adventure that most folks will only read about in fabulous literature. We were heading out to harvest our Christmas tree.

It all began in the tiny little Sweetwater general store the year before. It was there that I bumped into Bill Stevens, a long-time resident and dear friend. I mentioned I would like to collect a Christmas tree that would fill up our living room and he had an idea. He shared as how he knew a reclusive fellah in a huge log home up beyond civilization, who might just be willing to let us venture up for the harvest, as long as we didn't bother him.

Good fortune! I had written an article for the local little newspaper, explaining how I came to wear a Miami Dolphins jersey on stage during my lectures. Turns out that the hermit, up on the mountain, had seen the article and was more than willing to share not only a tree but a warmup beverage and a howdy. For the record, this tough-as-nails mountain man was one of the coolest guys we ever met. During our first handshake, I realized that his hand was so big, it wrapped all the way around mine.

In that blinding snow, we cut a nineteen-foot Douglas Fir and secured a friendship with the hermit. Turns out, his place was just above ours and we accepted an invitation to take our snow machine up to his home to watch a Super Bowl. His name was Jake Scott (R.I.P.). He had been a free safety for the Miami Dolphins, MVP of Super Bowl VII, and part of the only undefeated team in NFL history. I loved that Harvest.

Tigger

Metamorphosis

With friends and even family members turning our backs on one another, hiding out in our pandemic cocoons, I am often asked about how we might ease our minds a bit. I find that a thank you list is a powerful and wonderful place to begin to pull ourselves out of our chrysalis.

Conversation: "Thank you!" "What for?" "Do I have to have a reason?" "People diss each other all the time with little reason. Why can't I appreciate you for no reason? Besides, if the Good Lord saw fit to grant us life and passage to this point, that seems reason enough to say thanks."

How long is your "mahalo" list? Five, ten, fifteen items? Perhaps it seems endless! Often, when we begin to compile a reminder list, it is usually an "I want," kind of inventory. That's fine. Like you, I'm a dreamer, but I have made a rather simple but profound discovery. As I have been surfing along through these eighty-two years, I have found that it isn't those things which I have acquired that give me the feeling of wealth and success, it is what I have been able to give away and share that brings the most glorious feeling.

So, let's make an exercise of head and heart and begin to list our gratitude: For people, places, thoughts, and things that bring a spark of joy. Moments and memories, family, and friends.

Have you ever seen a video of a caterpillar in metamorphosis? In our western world we most often think of the monarch, the king of butterflies, its lowly beginning and glorious conclusion. It is written: "What the caterpillar calls the end of the world, the master calls a butterfly!" With profound respect for your faith, I plan to begin my list with a hearty thank you to our creator for the gift of our life and time. So, here's a butterfly kiss and my thanks to you.

A grateful Tiggerpillar

Bob

This morning our MacDonald Ranch was hot. Not Santa Barbara hot, 72 and misty, not Manhattan hot, 92 and sticky, but Las Vegas hot, 110 in the shade with no escape. So, at the conclusion of my morning walk, I was more than ready for a cold shower! Standing in the altogether, just about to step into that refreshing cascade, my wife called out, in a very excited voice, "Bobcat!" The next thing I knew, she was rushing into my bathroom, iPhone cam running, and I grabbed a towel. "Bobcat," she repeated, and I understood. She had spotted an unusual creature in our yard and wanted to share it with me. "Bobcat!"

As I grabbed my camera and raced to our back slider, I spotted a tawny creature moving from left to right, across the desert just beyond our patio. But this was no Bobcat, it was a coyote on the hunt, no doubt for his breakfast and my camera was rolling. Perhaps Sharon was mistaken about the kind of animal she had seen. To my left I saw my bride's camera up and filming another golden critter resting in the shade beneath our tree. It was indeed a beautiful, robust, and healthy-looking Bobcat. We both steadied our cameras and set to work, seriously filming this lounging beauty on our patio. As my readers can attest, our little monastery is often frequented by wild and wonderful creatures. Quail, chipmunks, coyotes, big horn sheep, rabbits, mourning doves, tarantulas, and a variety of snakes but a Bobcat was a rare, elusive, and welcomed visitor. Driven by the intense heat and her thirst, she had invaded our space for a splash of shade and sip of precious water.

At first our new and mysterious friend seemed to pay us no mind. Simply licking her paws and cleaning her face in the manner of any domestic feline, but finally, she turned to look over her shoulder directly at us and as if it were an afterthought she rose, shook out her coat and headed off into the wilds of our desert world. I wondered how my wife, a confirmed city girl, had known that this was a Bobcat and so I asked... Her reply, "I just looked at his name tag!"

Tigger

Neighbors and the Universe

He came quietly up to my perch on the top of my mountain. In a soft and sincere voice, he asked, "are you the author?" So began my friendship with our neighbor Mike. Here is Mike's wise and witty response to my recent Fibonacci Desert Wind.

Tigger-Doug: You have hit on a subject that I share. With both my parents being Italian Immigrants, I grew up among uncles, aunts, and cousin paisans... mi Familia. We all came from monster vegetable and fruit tree gardens on the Niagara Peninsula, where we didn't have a blade of grass in our back yard. We spent our summer evenings looking out from our covered porch, sipping homemade wine and sharing stories. When visitors came to call, they never left without being given a large paper bag full of freshly picked escarole, beans, tomatoes, and greens.

I remember well, my kind and gentle uncle, Remigio Lostraco, a former young loyal soldier in Mussolini's army and subsequent German prisoner of war. When I asked him why he didn't have any flowers in his garden... His response with an incredulous look on his face was, "Venanzio, whya woulda youa plant flowers... you can no eata flowers!"

So today, here in Canada, I have my monster vegi garden, in our back yard. Currently I am busy picking zucchini, potatoes, tomatoes, pole beans and swiss chard. My wife Helen is canning and freezing away. I plant, as in the old days, way more than we need, so we can provide fresh vegi-care for our neighbors, friends, and kids.

Like you, I am impressed with the prevalence of the Fibonacci sequence in nature. Each tomato bunch, the plant leaves, and petals, all seem to form in 3-5-7-9 bunches. That is why a four-leaf clover is such a curiosity. My T.D. Waterhouse, direct trading platform, has a Fibonacci retracement with fans and time zones for predicting stock market movement. This connection is based on the principle that our human brains are based on mathematical sequences. It makes you wonder if some highly intellectual being is out there working on achieving his or her PhD in physics with a billion-year test tube mathematical experiment, titled the Universe Thesis.

Mike and Tigger

Toast

In the classic comedy film, "Ghost Busters," Bill Murray, AKA Peter Venkman, looks dismissively at Gozer, the devil woman with the bloodshot eyes and declares: "This chick is toast!" Then he and his associates unleash their protein pack weapons, cross their beams, and terminate her existence. What would the world be like without toast?

In the thirty-one years that my bride and I have been together, we have never had a toaster. Our little Kitchen Aid toaster-oven has served us quite well. Although the design of our broiler seems to do the job, it is almost impossible to read the information on the controls. So, after turning up the rheostat on our kitchen lighting, unleashing my railroad flashlight, putting on my readers and getting down on bended knee, I can just barely launch my lunch.

In a pre-covid discussion with friends, over a glass of fine wine, I declared my love for toast: rye, sourdough, seven grain wheat, and cinnamon. You bake it and I will eat it! These bright young colleagues of ours came completely unglued at the thought of toast lovers, such as we, living all of these years with either under or over- cooked bread. They nearly burst a gasket laughing at our response when questioned, that we had no toaster anywhere in our home, garage, or storage unit. I covered the embarrassing moment by bragging about our superior nachos, toasted cheese sandwiches, and quiche.

On our next visit, these fine folks arrived with a neatly wrapped gift package. It seems that whatever age or station in life we reach, it is always a joy to open a gaily wrapped parcel. Imagine our surprise on opening to find that we were at last, the proud owners of a shiny new Sunbeam two-piece toaster. It has been a revelation and a celebration. No knobs to twirl, no gauges or timers to set, just drop in the gift of wonder, listen to the sweet ticking sound and await the "pop" that brings forth the Golden Brown treasure to be shared by all within the house. Oh, how large we shall become, savoring this gift.

Tigger

Tandem

Afternoon is their favorite time. I usually hear them calling, before I see them. They seem to rise up out of the mountain top with the setting sun behind them. They are highlighted by a golden silhouette and more than once, their dance has brought tears to my eyes. The inky-black crows who share our canyon, are graceful, powerful, and definitely connected.

Do you share a relationship? I do and I have always sought ways to build, to bond, to enhance our connection. It is in times together, that we find those tandem moments. Reading a book, sharing a film, laughing at a television show, taking a walk, sharing a worship experience, shopping, dining, loading, or emptying the dishwasher... All of these simple adventures offer a chance for tandem flight.

Although, once my wife showed me the proper way to load our dishwasher, we truly share all of the above adventures. For us, there is one activity that gives us the chance to learn, practice and improve our tandemness. We dance! Although our dance club activities are on covid hold and our travels to championship competitions are held in abeyance, we continue to dance in our living room, down the hall, in the laundry room and on the back patio. We may be on hold just now, but the vaccine is upon us and one day very soon we will be in our buggy heading off to the fourth-of-July Swing Dance Championships, in Phoenix, AZ.

That means that we have some choices. One, we could quit west coast swing dancing completely, climb into our rockers, or two, we could arrive at the Camelback Marriott, in Scottsdale, with some new moves in our repertoire physically, mentally, and spiritually ready to hit the dance floor. Tigger has always been off his rocker!

A Face in the Crowd

I t's been a long time and a million miles since that day. I have always believed that it is not the speaker or the performer that makes a show great... It is always the audience! We were in Sioux Falls, South Dakota and chosen as I was to be the opening speaker, I sat behind the curtains of the beautiful university auditorium, listened to the intro music, and said my prayers. When the curtains opened, I could not have imagined what would become of this moment.

My talk was titled the Challenge of Success, and the response from the audience was a presenter's dream. Together we laughed, cried, and cheered until we filled the room with a mighty, joyful noise. Having been an attendee at many a seminar, I know that each guest in every seat before me has their own thoughts, hopes dreams and challenges. Having had the good fortune of not only dreaming but figuring out how to turn my dreams into realities, it was my honor to be sharing that story and that pathway.

I try to bring the unvarnished truth to our guests, and it was that honesty that opened the door to a lifelong friendship. I spoke frankly: "Like you, I have lived a life with its share of both joys and heartbreaks." In the story, I revealed how our family had lost our daughter in a traffic accident and how that tragedy had shaped our lives and called me to be a better man.

We never know what those before us have experienced or are going through. That is why the heartfelt truth is so precious. Dead center in the audience, about ten rows back was a lady who had lost her son in a boating accident. At the break, we shared a hug and a tear. She and her husband became lifelong friends. Now, a half-century later as I write this desert wind, I look down on my desk to view the autumn leaves which are an annual birthday token from Grayce, Ron and Minnesota. That evening as I performed the concert, I sang my song, "A Butterfly for Bucky..." with tears in my eyes.

Tigger

One Day

W hat you are about to read is not at all how this Desert Wind began. Before posting these Chronicles, I often try to confirm that what I am writing is true, accurate and entertaining. I also love to share a song or message that inspires my beloved readers. That is how this DWC came to be.

Do you have a favorite type of music? An era, a decade, a sound, a voice, or a style that moves you? Is there a group or a song that takes you back to a time and place? It is said that the best time machine is a record. You remember, the little black vinyl disks with a hole in the middle and the memories of your life and loves captured in those barely visible grooves. You remember, don't you?

One of the songs that takes me back to that moment was titled "One Day," and when I first heard those voices and lyrics, I was hooked. *"One day, I'm sure we'll all be happy, peace will soon find everyone!"* They called themselves by their real names Batdorf and Rodney and I thought that they were terrific. They seemed to be singing and saying how they felt. I was so happy to be a part of promoting their music for Atlantic Records.

I write today about the deep feeling that there are so many songs of yesterday and today we need to hear and heed now! After the violence, hatred and the pandemic that has torn us to shreds, it would seem that we need Batdorf and Rodney today more than ever. Youtube it: "One Day," Batdorf and Rodney. *"Let's make the best of things, I know we can get by...Try and keep our heads up high."*

John Batdorf was and is as kind as his music. I know that because I recently reached out for his approval and permission to publish this Desert Wind. He said yes!

Tigger

https://johnbatdorfmusic.com/shop/
https://youtube.com/user/sing4do

Magic Carpet (Part One)

Beneath a warm California morning sun, we are seated at the world-famous restaurant, Casa La Golondrina. With the mariachi sounds of "Malagueña Salerosa," drifting over our perfect margaritas and fragrant arroz con pollo, our eyes can sweep across two-hundred-fifty years of California's rich history. We are seated at an outdoor table on Olvera Street, or El Pueblo De Los Angeles, the birthplace of the City of Angels. This is certainly a fine beginning to our most romantic journey.

Across the busy, traffic filled Alameda Street, stands the beautiful Union Station. It is the largest passenger station in the western United States and is our point of embarkation. Opened in nineteen-thirty-nine, it is a fine artistic example of Mission Revival and Art Deco architecture. From the tow-headed toddler who first boarded the Southwest Chief, to the great grandfather that I am today, I have observed many movie stars, both past and present climbing on and off the east bound train that will be our "magic carpet made of steel." Brunch over, we cross the busy thoroughfare where we are met by a red cap who has stored our luggage and will transport and escort us to our sleeping car.

On board our accommodations are classy and comfortable. We have reservations for a Super Liner, Deluxe Bedroom. Included, adult size bunk beds which fold up, to clear the way for a fine drawing room with reclining chairs and a fold down table for cocktails and snacks. Our train offers a lounge car with a glass dome, from which we can watch America drift by and a dining car that smells as fine as our freshly prepared meals taste.

All Abooooooooooard! The conductor, or Chief, beckons stragglers to get on board. The slightest movement is proof positive that we are on our way to Chicago. ROUTE 66, Sing it backwards and you have a route map for our journey. Tigger's happy place, Car 3100 Bedroom #4. (To be continued...)

Magic Carpet (Part Two)

His little face is pressed against the window of his parent's car. This is the little boy's first road trip to Las Vegas. He has already seen so many wonderful things, but this is simply the best. His dream of a train ride is tantalizingly close, as if he could run along and jump on board. The bright and shining *Southwest Chief* is rolling along beside them, at least for now.

Across the inland empire and up through the Cajon Pass, the silver compliment of the beautiful magic carpet snakes its way through the history of early California. Two powerful diesel engines, a baggage car, a dining car, three coaches and two superliner sleeping cars, make up the train. The boy can see them all.

The family car headed into Nevada, has provided a perfect window for the little face that looks out upon the silver wonder. How many times in my young life was I the one looking out through my family's car window and wishing? This time I am in my sleeping car, waving out at the young viewer. With a last longing look, the boy and his family continue north and his dream turns west toward Chicago.

Any station along this route is a wonder. (Route 66) From the smallest to the grandest. Victorville, Needles, Kingman, Williams, (The Gateway to the Grand Canyon) and ahead, in Arizona, at seven-thousand feet, the beautiful Flagstaff Station. In winter blizzards and summer heat, I have lifted my bags on board and departed from this historic station many times. (FLG)

My breakfast in the dining car is a plate full of bacon, eggs, and toast. The coffee is a hot and a perfect accompaniment to the ponderosa pines that dance in the wind outside my view window. Albuquerque next!

I have always enjoyed the stop in ABQ. It is a fuel and "scrub up the train" stop, so there is time to get off, enjoy some fry bread and shop at the Navajo jewelry stands. The silver is as shiny as our freshly washed train and the turquoise is as blue as the sky above us. Two thousand I-phone steps later and quite refreshed, I step back into my car, enter my deluxe bedroom and begin to dream of the gorgeous Kansas City Station (KCY) that lies ahead.

Tigger

Magic Carpet (Part Three)

Santa Fe. Nestled in the Sangre De Christo foothills, "The City Different," certainly lives up to its nom du plume. For me, the name conjures up cattle drives, cowboy songs, marvelous cuisine, and world class artwork. The station for the city of Santa Fe is Lamy (LMY) and as we stop briefly and then roll quickly on, it is clear that the pandemic has touched more than just big cities.

Outside my window, as we transition from high desert chaparral to two needle pine, rocky mountain juniper, blue spruce and gambel oak, we are on our way, gliding past the final sights of New Mexico and heading for Raton Pass. Colorado here we come!

Located on the New Mexico/Colorado border, Raton Pass is the gateway between the Sangre De Christo range and the Rocky Mountains. At seven thousand eight hundred feet, it is the highest point on the Santa Fe Trail and our entry to the great plains of America.

I am always astonished at my fellow travelers reaching this point on the route who, with a sullen look on their faces exclaim, "This is the boring part!" Forgive me but for those who have eyes, the view on the way to Kansas City includes sweeping plains, huge thunderheads, beautiful sun rises and sunsets, not to mention antelope, deer, bear, coyotes, hawks, and eagles. Did I mention

Dodge City? The depot is located on Wyatt Earp Boulevard, at the former El Vaquero Harvey House. Even if you are remaining on board, the memory of the Harvey Girls and the view out your window is romantic and wonderful. The train chief (Conductor) calls out "Hutcheson, Hutcheson next stop." The call reminds me I have beloved friends in that town and that the mighty Kansas City Station lies just ahead.

(KCY) Can a place where the train stops, also be a fine restaurant, planetarium, science city, live theater, movie theater, the KC Rail experience, and model train exhibit? The answer is a resounding yes! I have done all of these and more but in part four, I would like to share two specific adventures before we pull out for Chicago. The first involves my wonderful friends from Hutcheson, and the second has to do with Christmas time on the Southwest Chief. To be continued...

Tigger

Magic Carpet (Part Four)

On one very special evening, in the autumn of the year, the Peel family from Hutcheson, invited me to join them, along with some family, friends and associates, for a wine and dinner event at Pierpont's fine restaurant in the heart of the Kansas City Union Station. This wondrous building, opened in 1914, began as a working train station through which hundreds of thousands of passengers arrived and departed. Countless World War II soldiers came through on troop trains, waving at the patriotic family's trackside, off to fight for our country. Farmers and families boarded the train here, on their way off to seek their fortune.

Peel "Senior," as we knew Bob, along with his son, both wine connoisseurs, were the perfect hosts for just such an evening. Imagine arriving in a limo or taxi at this historic site, in black and white attire, to share an evening of the finest wine and Kansas beef, to the background of laughter and stories of the masters. It might as well have been the nineteen forties from the look and sound of us.

Because I have enjoyed train travel throughout my life, folks have always asked me, what is the best route and when is the best time for rail travel? Easy answer, *anywhere* at Christmastime. If you are riding along with us, on these Magic Carpet chapters, then all you need to do is ad Christmas décor. From the Los Angeles

Union station, all the way to KC, the folks who live along the tracks have put out their best. Once you leave the dining car and head back to your accommodations, as the sun goes down the red and green lights come on. Whatever decorations you might find in your neighborhood or city, you now find gliding by outside your picture window. In every field, farm, and woodland, like fireflies, the magic comes and goes until you find yourself mesmerized. It becomes hard to have your bed turned down and you hesitate to climb in and close your eyes. But wait...There's more.

Each year at the holidays, Kansas City Union Station transforms itself into a Christmas delight! The grand plaza of the station becomes a holiday walk through village, featuring dozens of decorated trees, forest friends and giant ornaments reflecting the glory of the seasons.With the voices of a local choir echoing in the ceiling, it is time to return to our Magic Carpet for the journey to the Windy City. (ORD)

Magic Carpet (Part Five)

What a wonderful place to be. In the midst of two wonderful destinations. Over my shoulder, the grand and beautiful Kansas City Station, and nine hours ahead, the huge, iconic Chicago Union Station. I am reminded of a story that I have told many times from the stage, about the young man sitting up on the bank of a country road, observing a chap walking by below. The traveler comes upon an old man seated along the roadside. "I say old man, what is the town like up ahead?" The old chap proceeds to ask, "What was the town like where you came from?" "Terrible," he replies, and the old fellow responds, "I think you will find the town up ahead pretty much the same..." As the young boy watches, a second wayfarer comes along in the same direction and repeats the dialogue with the old man. The old fellow repeats his question about the town from whence the second traveler has come. This time the response is just the opposite. "Wonderful place, happy cheerful people." "Then" continued the old man by the roadside, "You will find the town up ahead much the same..."

Now the young observer finds this strange and confronts the old fellow by the road. "Excuse me sir, but you just told one traveler that the town ahead would be terrible and the other, that the town ahead would be great, what's the scoop?" The old man shifted the piece of farm grass in his teeth, took a deep breath and replied, "Young fellah, after living these ninety years, I have come to know that how you leave a town, is pretty much how you are going to find the next one!"

For nearly a century the Chicago Union Station has been the railroad hub for the nation. With three million Amtrak passengers a year and thirty-five million Metra commuters each year, Union is the third busiest station in the country. From Jersey Mikes to Robinsons Ribs, what you want baby, you got it! An incredible variety of foods and services are yours for the exploring.

Although we never really leave the railroad behind, it is time to head for a spot where we can unwind the tales of our recent ride along the silver rails of The Southwest Chief. As we step down onto the platform to exit our *Magic Carpet,* we leave our bags, with Geno, the Red Cap. It is time to walk the three blocks to *Berghoff,* our favorite post train ride Restaurant. Old Fashions, stories, and dinner and at seven. We have you joining us...

Peace

One million miles! That is a lot of flying, or as John Denver put it "a long time to hang in the sky." I truly loved my travels and those moments in flight when I was granted the gift of time to read, to listen and to meditate.

For all of those million miles, and that was only on United, my favorite seat is, was and will always be "1A." It was in that seat that I first experienced the artistry of the Japanese Artist, Missa Johnouchi. Born in nineteen-sixty, she is a composer, pianist, conductor, and singer, who creates Asian style new age music. Missa was named UNESCO Artist for *Peace* in August two-thousand-six. Since, Missa Johnouchi has been accompanied by the Orchestra Nationale de Paris in creating her exquisite albums.

As one era, the days of international travel and performance, with luxurious hotels, fine food and fabulous audiences crash into the days, weeks, and months of pandemic, I find myself, as I did at thirty-seven-thousand feet, in the first-class cabin of that Boeing seven-forty-seven, reaching out for a moment's peace. I long for a hug, a sense of belonging, and a feeling of peace.

That is where music rises up to pour over my fevered brow like an island waterfall, bringing me comfort and connection to places near and far, people known and yet to know. Though there are many, my favorite piece, or "peace" of Missa's music, surrounds me like a warm Japanese bath on a foggy San Francisco evening in the Miyako Hotel, Japan Town.

Whenever we share a song with trusted friends, we always take the chance that our dear ones will not find favor in the sound, the music, or the artist we have chosen. This one is worth the risk. I choose "Marco Polo," from her "Asian Blossoms," Album, as my overture to sharing a new artist with my beloved readers.

The choice is ours; surround ourselves with today's madness or the music of our choosing. The characters at the end of this story mean "PEACE."

Tiger-san

平和

Made in the USA
Monee, IL
13 April 2025

15698211R00098